C000140600

Fortress • 44

American Coastal Defenses 1885–1950

T McGovern & B Smith • Illustrated by Peter Bull

Series editors Marcus Cowper and Nikolai Bogdanovic

First published in 2006 by Osprey Publishing
Midland House, West Way, Botley, Oxford OX2 0PH, UK
443 Park Avenue South, New York, NY 10016, USA
E-mail: info@ospreypublishing.com

© 2006 Osprey Publishing Limited

All rights reserved. Apart from any fair dealing for the purpose of private study,
research, criticism or review, as permitted under the Copyright, Designs and Patents
Act, 1988, no part of this publication may be reproduced, stored in a retrieval system,
or transmitted in any form or by any means, electronic, electrical, chemical, mechanical,
optical, photocopying, recording or otherwise, without the prior written permission of
the copyright owner. Enquiries should be addressed to the Publishers.

ISBN 10: 1 84176 922 3
ISBN 13: 978 1 84176 922 6

Cartography: Map Studio, Romsey, UK
Design: Ken Vail Graphic Design, Cambridge, UK
Typeset in Monotype Gill Sans and ITC Stone Serif
Index by Alison Worthington
Originated by United Graphic, Singapore
Printed and bound in China through Bookbuilders

06 07 08 09 10   10 9 8 7 6 5 4 3 2 1

A CIP catalog record for this book is available from the British Library.

FOR A CATALOG OF ALL BOOKS PUBLISHED BY OSPREY MILITARY AND AVIATION
PLEASE CONTACT:

Osprey Direct, c/o Random House Distribution Center, 400 Hahn Road, Westminster,
MD 21157
Email: info@ospreydirect.com

Osprey Direct UK, P.O. Box 140, Wellingborough, Northants, NN8 2FA, UK
E-mail: info@ospreydirect.co.uk

www.ospreypublishing.com

Dedication

This book is respectfully dedicated to our fathers, Emerson Smith
and Terry McGovern, who took their sons to their first forts and
encouraged their interest in fortifications.

Acknowledgments

We acknowledge with gratitude the tolerance of our wives, who
have put up with our all-consuming interest, watched our slides,
listened to our discussions, and accompanied us to isolated
fortifications spots around the world.
Members of the Coast Defense Study Group (www.cdsg.org) have
contributed unselfishly to this project, especially Mark Berhow,
Joel Eastman, Gregory Hagge, David Kirchner, and Glen Williford.
Their contributions are gratefully acknowledged. Any remaining
errors are solely the responsibility of the authors. We also offer
special thanks to Nikolai Bogdanovic and Marcus Cowper at Ilios
Publishing for efforts in creating the Fortress series and for
editing this Osprey book.

The purpose of this book is to encourage readers to visit these
sites to discover for themselves the tangible remains of America's
coastal fortifications. We hope it will make clearer to them what
they see, while explaining what is no longer there to be seen.

Terrance McGovern
1700 Oak Lane
McLean VA 22101 USA
tcmcgovern@att.net
tmcgovern@icfconsulting.com

Bolling Smith
bollingsmith@hotmail.com

Artist's note

Readers may care to note that the original paintings from which
the color plates in this book were prepared are available for
private sale. All reproduction copyright whatsoever is retained by
the Publishers. All enquiries should be addressed to:

Peter Bull Art Studio
8 Hurstwood Road
Bredhurst
Gillingham
ME7 3JZ
United Kingdom

The Publishers regret that they can enter into no correspondence
upon this matter.

The Fortress Study Group (FSG)

The object of the FSG is to advance the education of the public in
the study of all aspects of fortifications and their armaments,
especially works constructed to mount or resist artillery. The FSG
holds an annual conference in September over a long weekend
with visits and evening lectures, an annual tour abroad lasting
about eight days, and an annual Members' Day.
The FSG journal FORT is published annually, and its newsletter
Casemate is published three times a year. Membership is
international. For further details, please contact:
The Secretary, c/o 6 Lanark Place, London W9 1BS, UK

The Coast Defense Study Group (CDSG)

The Coast Defense Study Group (CDSG) is a non-profit
corporation formed to promote the study of coast defenses and
fortifications, primarily but not exclusively those of the United
States of America; their history, architecture, technology, and
strategic and tactical employment. Membership in the CDSG
includes four issues of the organization's two quarterly
publications, the Coast Defense Journal and the CDSG Newsletter.
For more information about the CDSG please visit www.cdsg.org
or to join the CDSG write to:
[Attn: Glen Williford] Coast Defense Study Group, Inc., 634 Silver
Dawn Court, Zionsville, IN 46077-9088, USA

Contents

Introduction   4

Chronology   8

American coastal defenses in the muzzle-loading era   9

The colonial and Revolutionary period • The First System 1794–1806 • The Second System 1807–15
The Third System 1816–67 • After the Civil War 1868–84

American coastal defenses during the Modern Era   12

Before the Endicott Board • The Endicott-Taft System 1885–1915 • Harbor defense between the wars 1916–36
World War II harbor defense 1937–45 • Postwar harbor defense 1945–50

Life in the coast artillery   17

Before World War I • Life during World War I • Life between the World Wars • The World War II experience

Coastal defense in the Modern Era   21

The framework of coast defense • Tactical and administrative organization • Land defense of seacoast forts

The fort   26

Endicott-Taft forts • Permanent structures • Cantonments and temporary non-tactical buildings
World War II coast artillery forts and reservations

Armament and batteries   30

Seacoast ammunition   45

US Army controlled submarine mines   46

The mines • Mine groups • Mine buildings • Mine flotilla

Fire control and position finding   51

Endicott-Taft fire control • Fire control between the World Wars • Fire control in World War II

Searchlights   57

General searchlight principles • Fixed searchlight projectors • Mobile searchlights

The forts today   59

Suggestions for visits

Recommended reading   61

Glossary   62

Abbreviations

Index   64

Introduction

From the very beginning, Americans had to defend themselves against seaborne threats. As its population grew, America's faith in its citizenry, coupled with geographic isolation, resulted in a small standing army, largely on the frontier. While a citizen army could repel invasion, assembling such an army at the point of attack would take time. Americans recognized the need to defend vulnerable points against sudden attack and to buy time for the nation to assemble its manpower. Furthermore, a field army, no matter how resolute, had neither the mobility nor the firepower to repel warships.

The result was an acknowledgment that America needed permanent fortifications to protect her seaports. While virtually every nation recognized the superiority of forts over ships and relied on fortifications to protect their harbors, America took to them with particular enthusiasm. They particularly suited the American character. It required little manpower except during time of war and did not threaten the liberties of a people raised to distrust standing armies. Equally important, coastal forts, rather than encouraging international conflicts, would deter them.

After the War of 1812, the Board of Engineers for Fortification set forth the basic aims of the fortification program (which became the Third System), which remained remarkably unchanged for over a century. The US Civil War demonstrated the vulnerability of the old masonry forts to land-based rifled guns, and by the 1880s, steam-powered ironclad warships with rifled guns had completely upset the relationship between forts and ships. America, however, still relied on seacoast weapons left over from the US Civil War.

With its navy neglected and its seacoast defenses all but abandoned, the American Congress finally created an inter-service committee in 1885 to examine the needs and means for defending the coast. The ensuing report of the "Endicott Board" established the Endicott Program, which in turn created the Endicott System, the basic pattern for American coast defenses until their demise after World War II. When modified by the Taft Board, this system became the Endicott-Taft System.

If the Third System had been extensive, the Endicott-Taft System was even more so. By the start of World War I, nearly a hundred forts and hundreds of gun and mortar batteries defended over 30 harbors, supported by submarine mines, searchlights, and all the other necessary appliances of war. It was the greatest defensive effort in the history of the country, and its remains still stand at virtually every significant harbor in the country. Compared to the older Third System works, however, the concrete batteries of the breech-loading era, less obvious and less intuitive, have for decades been shrouded in ignorance and misperception. Even their date has often been misjudged, since concrete can belie its age. Only in recent years have the batteries and structures of the Modern Era (1885 to 1950) begun to receive the historical attention they deserve.

As America again moved toward war in 1940, a systematic program (which became known at the 1940 Program) was adopted to modernize the coast defenses, replacing older works with new ones that were more powerful yet required fewer men. As these new batteries were completed, the older guns were scrapped. At the same time, the war increasingly turned in America's favor, and many new batteries were cancelled before completion. The war ended as America was completing an unrivaled system of coast defenses, but victory eliminated the need. Within a few years America's coastal defenses were dismantled, its guns cut up for scrap.

Their scenic locations near large cities have made these defenses visible to many casual visitors. The nature of fortifications, their permanence and resistance to destruction, has allowed them to withstand both natural elements and economic development. Among the most prominent surviving artifacts of American military history, they continue to inspire public interest. This interest, however, is seldom matched by available information. Far too many visitors leave with no clear understanding of the forts, when they were built, or how they functioned.

Today, interest continues to grow, as the forts of America's Modern Era are finally beginning to be recognized as historic. A previous Osprey volume, *American Civil War Fortifications: Coastal Brick and Stone Forts* – Fortress No. 6, dealt with the masonry forts of the Third System. The present volume introduces the forts of the Modern Era, characterized by breech-loading guns and concrete batteries, and how they protected the nation from 1885 to 1950.

After World War I, the US Coast Artillery Corps acquired additional functions in addition to harbor defense, most notably antiaircraft defense. These functions, however, are outside the scope of this volume. The defenses described are those of the United States, and all references to army or navy are to the US Army and the US Navy, as well as to their various departments, boards, and corps, unless otherwise specified. Additionally all references to Congress are to the US Congress, the legislative and funding branch of the US Federal Government.

Battery Harris, Fort Tilden, NY, before 1938 (above) and after 1997 (below). This battery for two M1919 16in. guns on BC M1919 was constructed with open emplacements for all-round fire in 1924, but during World War II each emplacement received its own casemate while keeping the battery's dispersed magazines and power houses. (NARA Cartographic and McGovern Collection)

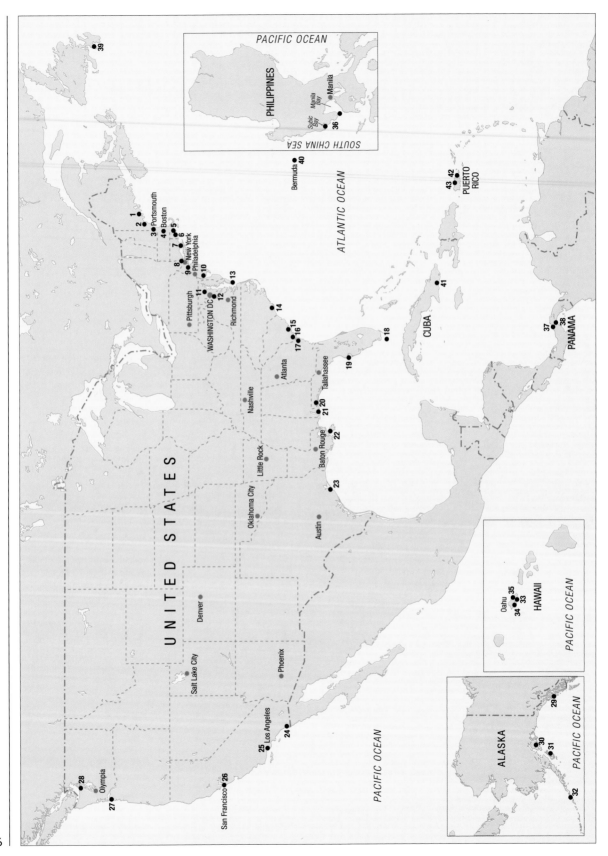

PACIFIC OCEAN

PHILIPPINES

Manila

Manila Bay

Subic Bay

36

SOUTH CHINA SEA

39

40 Bermuda

ATLANTIC OCEAN

43 42 PUERTO RICO

1
2
3 Portsmouth
4 Boston
5
6
7 New York
8
9 Philadelphia
10
11 Pittsburgh
12 WASHINGTON DC
13 Richmond
14
15
16
17
18
19 Tallahassee
20
21 Atlanta
22 Baton Rouge
23
24
25 Los Angeles
26 San Francisco
27
28 Olympia

Nashville

Little Rock

Oklahoma City

Austin

Denver

Salt Lake City

Phoenix

41

CUBA

37
38 PANAMA

UNITED STATES

PACIFIC OCEAN

Oahu
34 35
33
HAWAII

PACIFIC OCEAN

ALASKA

29
30 31
32

PACIFIC OCEAN

6

powered steel guns, although the model years do not reflect actual final approval and production.

While barbette carriages resembling those for big muzzle-loading guns were available, the pressing need was for some means of protecting the guns and crews. Naval tactics at the time emphasized approaching forts closely, where the ships' preponderance of light weapons and elevated firing positions could disable the gun crews. To counter this threat, some European countries adopted domed iron turrets. Although the Endicott Board recommended turrets for key locations, the expense proved prohibitive. The engineers built one gun-lift battery, which protected the guns and crew during loading by lowering the guns on large platform lifts.

The issue was finally resolved by the Buffington-Crozier disappearing carriage, which both hid and protected the weapon and its crew behind a thick parapet. By 1896, in addition to several mortar batteries being completed, disappearing gun batteries were under construction at a number of locations. Although funding varied considerably, the Spanish-American War caused panicked fear of a Spanish fleet descending on unprotected coastal cities. Appropriations surged, for both temporary and permanent works. At the same time, the army began to consider how to direct and control the new weapons, and the first fire-control stations were constructed at the turn of the century.

In 1901, Congress authorized a major reorganization of the artillery. It had consisted of seven regiments, each containing heavy (seacoast) and light (field) batteries. With the companies widely spread, the regiments had been unable to exercise effective control, either administratively or tactically. The artillery was now organized into an Artillery Corps, with 30 batteries of field artillery and 126 companies of coast artillery. Companies were allocated to individual harbors as new batteries were completed. At the same time, the Corps of Engineers transferred responsibility for the development and use of submarine mines to the Artillery Corps.

In 1905, President Theodore Roosevelt appointed another board, headed by Secretary of War William H. Taft, to review and update the Endicott Program in view of the advances in electrical technology and the need to defend overseas bases acquired from Spain. The 1906 "Taft Report" recommended new sites for defenses made possible by the increased range of modern guns, and for the new territories, including Panama, Hawaii, and the Philippines. In addition, the board emphasized electricity, searchlights, and modern fire control. Gun and battery design continued to evolve, now being more properly the Endicott-Taft System.

In 1907, Congress again reorganized the artillery, this time into two separate branches, the field artillery and a Coast Artillery Corps (CAC), which was increased

LEFT M1905 6in. gun on a DC M1903 at Battery Chamberlain, Fort Scott, CA, in 1982; today it is part of the Golden Gate NRA. Battery Chamberlain was built in 1904 as part of the Endicott-Taft System to defend San Francisco Bay from torpedo boats and minesweepers. This 6in. gun, originally located in a training battery at West Point, was reinstalled in 1976. (McGovern Collection)

RIGHT Battery Gunnison/New Peck, Fort Hancock, NJ, from 500ft in 1997. Battery Gunnison was constructed for two 6in. disappearing guns in 1905, but in 1943 it was rebuilt for two M1900 6in. guns on BC M1900 from Battery Peck and renamed Battery New Peck. It served as an examination battery until 1946. Two guns were reinstalled in 1976 when the fort became part of Gateway NRA. (McGovern Collection)

to 170 companies to man the expanded mine program and the defenses being constructed overseas. The next decade was something of a golden era for the CAC, as batteries were completed and improved fire control was installed. World War I, however, disrupted everything, forcing the CAC to concentrate on raising and training heavy artillery regiments for service with the American Expeditionary Force in France.

Harbor defense between the wars 1916–36

The nadir of the coast artillery was from the end of World War I until the country began to rearm for the next world war. The wartime strength of the CAC was repeatedly slashed, while the few men left were also responsible for antiaircraft and heavy artillery. During the 1920s and early 30s, the CAC had only caretaker troops for most of its continental defenses. The continental units devoted much of their energy to training the National Guard and Organized Reserve regiments that would provide the bulk of the initial manpower for the defenses in case of war. Most training was limited to the overseas defenses, which had greater manpower since they had no National Guard to rely on. During the same period, the CAC began to integrate mobile railway and tractor-drawn guns into the harbor defenses.

World War II harbor defense 1937–45

As the 1930s came to a close, increased funding allowed the CAC to begin to return its batteries to service, with a meager amount for new construction. By 1940, with war on the horizon, the National Guard was called into federal service and the CAC finally began to shake off its doldrums. When America entered World War II, the CAC intensified its efforts to reinforce Hawaii, organize harbor defenses in Alaska, and provide defenses for Atlantic and Caribbean bases acquired for destroyers. The CAC, however, increasingly focused on its antiaircraft role, even as it built new series of seacoast batteries at home and abroad.

As the war began to turn in the Allies' favor, the need for coast defense decreased, just as the new batteries, intended to decrease manpower requirements, came into service. Coast defense manpower steadily decreased, as able-bodied men were transferred to the mobile army and replaced, if at all, by men less physically capable.

Postwar harbor defense 1945–50

By the war's end, nearly 200 modern and modernized batteries had been completed in the continental United States at a cost of $220 million. While this only represented about half the installations projected in the 1940 Program, they still comprised the most powerful coast defenses in the history of the nation, if not the world. Developments in military technology and tactics

Casemated battery

The US Army's 1940 Modernization Program for coast defenses resulted in construction of casemated batteries for 16in. guns on barbette carriages and the secondary batteries for 6in. guns on shielded barbette carriages. San Francisco was a vital harbor and the growing Japanese threat in the 1930s caused the army to select this harbor defense to receive two 16in. batteries, one on each side of the Golden Gate. Fort Funston at Lake Merced was selected for the southern battery. This prototype battery design consisted of a pair of 16in. guns with enormous casemates 600ft apart, connected by galleries housing the ammunition magazines, electrical power plants, and storage and operating facilities. The entire battery structure, designed to withstand battleship projectiles or aerial bombs, was roofed along its full length by 8–10ft of densely reinforced concrete and up to 20ft of earth. Battery Richmond P. Davis, constructed at Fort Funston between 1937 and 1939, mounted two 16in. MkII Mod1 navy guns on M2 barbette carriages. The battery today is open to the public as part of the Golden Gate NRA, NPS.

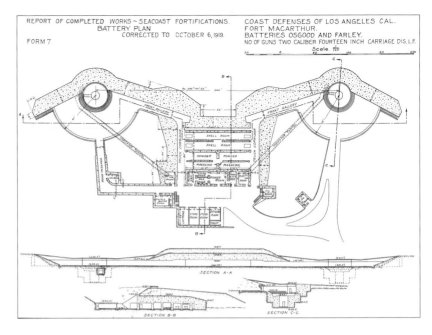

RIGHT General plan and section for Batteries Osgood and Farley at Fort MacArthur, CA. This Corps of Engineers RCW drawing from 1919 shows the layout for two 14in. disappearing batteries. (NARA Textual, RG 77, Entry 1007)

during World War II had changed the concept of coast defense. Before World War II, coast defense had concentrated on defending harbors, since invasions required harbors for support. Modern amphibious warfare and the new tactics and equipment for landing and sustaining an army over a beach made those assumptions obsolete.

While prewar planners took air attack much more seriously than is commonly believed, both the equipment and techniques of air attack made great advances during the war, and the most likely threat to harbors was no longer from battleships but aircraft carriers, far beyond the range of coastal guns. The US Navy was now supreme at sea, and no nation could build a hostile fleet in the foreseeable future. Coupled with this was an intense postwar drive to economize.

The end of World War II found all coast defenses except a few 90mm anti-motor torpedo boat (AMTB) batteries on caretaking status. The CAC initially proposed a massive program of big-gun turrets, and even considered emplacing entire warships in concrete as fixed defenses. When these were rejected, the CAC proposed to preserve the structures and equipment, on which so much money had been spent, at a small fraction of their purchase price. The army, however, was unwilling to spend anything at all to preserve coast defenses in the absence of any foreseeable threat, and flatly rejected the proposals. Between 1946 and 1948, a few batteries started during the war were completed, but soon they and the other batteries were disposed of. By 1949, the last guns were scrapped and the process was complete. In 1950, the remaining harbor defense commands were disbanded and the Coast Artillery Corps was abolished, its antiaircraft units recombined with the field artillery. After 150 years as a national military priority, permanent coastal fortifications ceased to exist.

The US Navy assumed responsibility for limited harbor defense, concentrating on the threat from submarines. The sole coast defense role envisaged by the army was the limited use of antiaircraft artillery as expeditionary harbor defenses. During the 1950s, this role faded and army coast defense finally disappeared.

BELOW Battery Lewis (BCN 116), Navesink Highland MR, NJ, from 500ft in 1997. Completed in 1944, this 100-Series battery housed two MkII ModI 16in. navy guns on BC M4 in protective casemates. The service gallery between the two guns connected with projectile and powder rooms, as well as the large power plant. (McGovern Collection)

Life in the coast artillery

A century ago, the army was sharply divided between officers and enlisted men, much more than today. For enlisted soldiers and non-commissioned officers (NCOs) assigned to gun companies, the pattern of life remained remarkably constant from 1885 through 1916, like life in any other army unit; the rhythm was much the same. The peacetime experience, of course, differed from wartime, and especially after World War I, there were significant differences between stateside and overseas duty.

Before World War I

While there were differences at individual posts, the pre-World War I experience for most coast artillery soldiers was similar. Married NCOs lived in quarters like those of the officers, but smaller and plainer. Single NCOs and enlisted men lived in barracks, which were the center of life. The soldiers bunked in squad rooms on the second floor, which also contained NCO rooms and often a barbershop. The ground floor contained the kitchen and mess hall, offices for company officers and NCOs, as well as recreation and reading rooms. The basement contained the latrines and showers, boiler room, and rooms for coal, commissary stores, and company equipment. Although there were sports, a post exchange, and perhaps a post library, soldiers spent most off-duty time in their barracks.

The day started when the bugler sounded "first call." At 5:30 AM in the summer and 6:30 in the winter, the company stood for reveille roll call in their dress blue uniforms, much more common then than now. In the course of the day, the men might change uniforms as often as five times. Breakfast was 15 minutes after reveille. The men had at least 20 minutes for breakfast and dinner, and 30 minutes for supper. After the men policed the barracks, they divided for training. The range, gun, and ammunition sections drilled separately, wearing the service uniform, khaki or olive wool or cotton. Enlisted men working around greasy equipment wore baggy fatigue uniforms over their service uniforms.

After drill, the men marched back for dinner at noon. Training occupied the first part of the afternoon; the men were usually dismissed in the middle of the afternoon. Supper could be between 5:00 and 6:30 PM. Retreat would be no later than sunset, with roll call formation and a parade, if there had been no parade at reveille. Afterwards, men not assigned to guard duty would be free to do as they chose. "Call to quarters" sounded at 10:45 PM, and with "taps" at 11:30, all lights not specifically authorized were extinguished, and soldiers not in bed were reported absent.

BOTTOM LEFT A gun section is performing maintenance on a 12in. disappearing gun at Battery Parrott, Fort Monroe, VA, in 1912. A large ramrod is sitting in an oil pan after the soldiers have swabbed the inside of the barrel and the breech block has been removed. (US Army Casemate Museum)

BOTTOM RIGHT The firing section prepares to ram a projectile into the breech of a 12in. disappearing gun at Battery DeRussey, Fort Monroe, VA, in 1912. Note the various roles of the manning detail, such as the gun pointer, truck detail (2), rammer detail (3), breech detail (2), range display board operator, and the deflection display board operator. (US Army Casemate Museum)

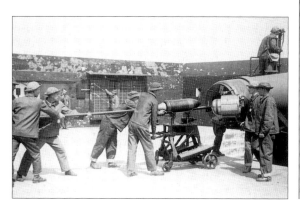

Drill and training depended on the season and the location. The year was divided into indoor and outdoor training seasons; their length related to the climate. Especially in northern forts, the winter was largely spent indoors, with emphasis on classroom training, both theoretical and practical. The subjects ranged from basic education to preparation for annual examinations for ratings.

While the coast artillery had NCOs like today, they were fewer and less well paid. They only held rank in their own units; if they transferred to another unit, they lost their rank. In addition to rank, ratings increased a soldier's pay. The first step was second class gunner. Once a first class gunner, soldiers could earn ratings in a number of specialties, such as gun pointer or plotter.

The outdoor training season, which might last nine months, was conducted at the battery. The gun and ammunition sections drilled repeatedly with dummy projectiles and dummy powder charges, striving for speed and consistency. Meanwhile, the range section tracked passing ships, plotted their positions, and calculated the firing data. The soldiers repeated this training day after day until it became second nature.

When the company graduated to sub-caliber training, they fired small guns mounted inside the big guns. This allowed the gun and range sections to practice as a unit, and stimulated interest by allowing the men to actually fire the guns inexpensively.

Finally, the company was ready for service target practice. The company officers checked and double-checked every piece of equipment, while NCOs insured each man knew his job perfectly, and could perform the duties of other men if called upon. On the specified day, a tug towed the target into the field of fire and the battery had a short time to fire the few rounds the cost-conscious US War Department allowed them. When scores were computed and analyzed, the company had a number to boast about or live down until the next service practice. While early regulations prescribed three service practices a year, economy soon reduced this to once or twice.

In addition, the army mandated field-training periods, when the coast artillery companies would leave their barracks and live in tents, practicing to serve as infantry. These periods culminated in the small-arms target practice, when the men fired their rifles and pistols for record.

In addition to official functions and training, the army stressed recreation. Sports, especially team sports, were encouraged, and units played each other as well as local civilian teams, providing both exercise and entertainment. Amateur theatrics, musical shows, and dances were frequent and popular. Companies celebrated holidays with banquets in the mess halls, lavishly decorated.

After the turn of the century, soldiers with a yen for the more exotic could serve tours in such overseas possessions as Panama, Hawaii, and the Philippines. While some soldiers disliked the separation from home and family, others enjoyed new surroundings, as well as the advantages of living amid a population that would perform mundane tasks for low wages. The lure of native women could add to the attraction. Hawaii was generally considered the best duty station in the coast artillery.

Overall, life in the peacetime coast artillery, like the rest of the army, was not overly strenuous. Training was relatively routine, free time was ample, a wide range of diversions was available, and with almost every necessity provided, soldiers' pay allowed a reasonable amount for enjoyment, with something to set aside for the next furlough.

Life during World War I

Life in the coast artillery changed radically during World War I. From an enlisted strength of 18,000 in

BELOW 10in. gun being removed from Fort Taylor, Key West, FL for use in France during World War I. These CAC and Ordnance officers are seen in February 1918 standing on a gun from Battery DeLeon after it was removed from its disappearing carriage. (NARA Still Pictures SC-6742)

1916, the CAC ballooned to 147,000 men by late 1918. With little threat of naval attack, the CAC concentrated on organizing, training, and equipping artillery regiments to man the heavy guns that had become so important in trench warfare.

The National Guard companies were called up immediately, joined by tens of thousands of volunteers and draftees. Units trained, divided, refilled with recruits, and repeated the cycle, as regiment after regiment was created. A number of artillery regiments from the CAC saw service in France, and more were in various stages of organization, training, or transportation when the Armistice abruptly ended the war.

ABOVE CMTC students pose on an M1888 10in. gun on a DC M1894 at Battery Cullum, Fort Pickens, FL, in July 1925. The CAC relied on the National Guard and Organized Reserve to man many of the batteries in wartime. (NARA Still Pictures SC-94867)

Life between the World Wars

With peace, manpower was slashed and units attempted to resume their peacetime routine. By the mid-1920s, manpower at the continental forts barely sufficed to maintain the guns, carriages, ammunition, and support equipment. A few posts with more men devoted much of their time to National Guard, Organized Reserve, CMTC, and ROTC training camps. Almost all tactical training took place overseas, in Panama, Hawaii, and the Philippines, where the army attempted to maintain enough manpower to conduct normal training. Although continental units were often a mere fraction of their wartime strength, caretaking duty was handled energetically, and morale was higher than might have been expected, perhaps because they had jobs and food during the Depression.

After about a decade, as manpower began to increase, equipment was rehabilitated and units began to resume tactical training. In 1940 and 1941, the National Guard entered federal service and began intensive training to perfect their skills. While often initially in tents, the guardsmen were soon quartered in new "mobilization-style" barracks. With the enactment of the peacetime draft, untrained "selectees" began to fill out the Regular Army and National Guard regiments. This necessitated another round of intensive training, and some National Guard regiments never quite recaptured the local feeling they once had. This training was still ongoing when the army found itself at war on December 7, 1941.

The World War II experience

With the coming of war, even more volunteers and draftees poured in, straining the existing facilities as more barracks and supporting structures were

LEFT M1905A2 6in. gun on shielded BC M1 at BCN 234, Fort Pickens, Santa Rosa Island, FL, in 1986. Two 200-series batteries were built as part of the 1940 Program to defend Pensacola, FL. This set of 6in. guns was moved here in 1976 from their original location at BCN 227, Fort John Custis, VA. (McGovern Collection)

Casemated gun emplacement of Battery Lewis (BCN 116), Navesink Highland Military Reservation, NJ, from 500ft in 1997. Completed in 1944, this 100-series battery housed two MkII 16in. navy guns. The gun barrel was installed and removed through the rear entrance. (McGovern Collection)

built. The days were much longer now; intensive training coupled with anxious duty manning the defenses. Only as time passed did many men begin to lose the apprehension of imminent invasion. As the war progressed favorably and the enemy naval threat diminished, more and more able-bodied men transferred out of the harbor defense units, replaced by less physically capable men, as the need for troops overseas increased. For the soldiers in the CAC, World War II, like the First World War, resulted in continual upheaval, as men transferred in and out and units were reorganized and redesignated. This state of constant change, coupled with the distinctly civilian outlook of the draftees, contrasted sharply with the cohesive attitude of the prewar coast artillery, professional but less hurried.

As fewer men were required, the coastal forts lost some of their sense of urgency. With peace, the army hurriedly demobilized, and the remaining men, now fewer than ever, once again concentrated on maintaining the guns and batteries. After only a few years, the last US harbor defenses closed and their men were reassigned. The coast artillery experience was finally over.

RIGHT Gun drill is under way on an M1900 6in. gun on BC M1900 at a temporary battery at Fort Story, VA, in March 1942. The coming of World War II resulted in the temporary placement of these guns, as new permanent batteries were constructed at Cape Henry on the Atlantic Ocean. (NARA Still Pictures No. 208-AA-125)

Coastal defense in the Modern Era

The framework of coast defense

Early in the 19th century, the Board of Engineers for Fortifications listed the defenses for the seaboard as the navy, the fortifications, interior communications by land and water, and a regular army with a well-organized militia, all combined into a single system. The navy was to be the first line, but since it had to carry the war to the enemy, forcing it to attempt to protect every vulnerable harbor would reduce it to impotence. In addition, the navy (inferior to the Royal Navy – its most likely enemy) needed yards for construction and repair, and harbors of rendezvous and refuge. The navy's freedom to engage in offensive warfare depended on the coast artillery, and it was one of the strongest advocates of coast defense.

Considering the needs of the country as a whole, and the navy in particular, the board set forth the purposes of the fortifications for over a hundred years:

1. To keep important harbors available to our navy, while closing them to an enemy.
2. To prevent the enemy from seizing positions where he could use his naval superiority to maintain himself and keep the entire coast in perpetual alarm.
3. To protect our principal cities from attack.
4. To protect the routes of interior navigation at their junction with the ocean.
5. To cover coastal shipping and interior navigation and assist the navy to protect this commerce.
6. To protect the great naval establishments.

Based on these objectives, the Endicott Board recommended defenses for the nation's seacoast. These were not actually "coast" defenses, but were limited to major harbors. This harbor defense depended on cooperation and coordination,

LEFT Three M1890 12in. BLM and four MC M1896M1 at Battery Anderson, Fort Monroe, VA, in 1918. The mortar detachment is adjusting the elevation and azimuth setting as per the indicator board located in the upper background. (US Army Casemate Museum)

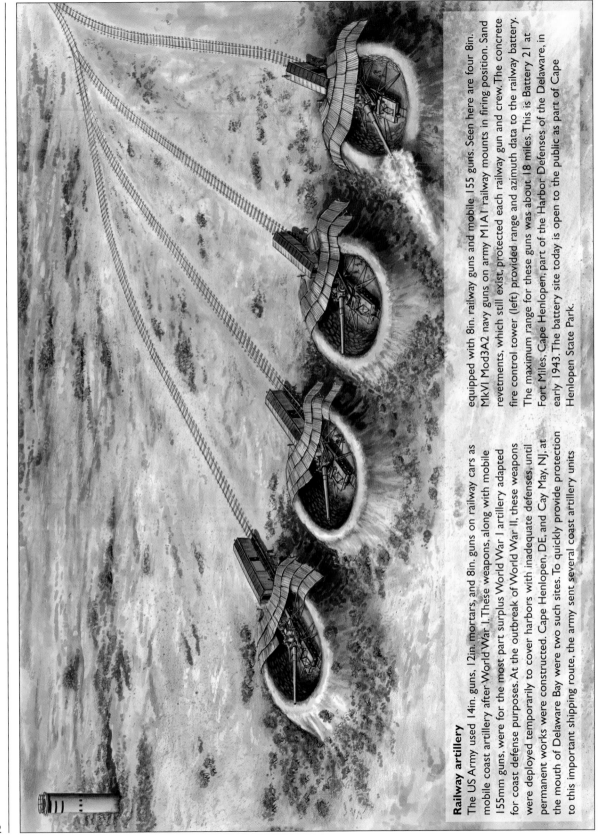

Railway artillery

The US Army used 14in. guns, 12in. mortars, and 8in. guns on railway cars as mobile coast artillery after World War I. These weapons, along with mobile 155mm guns, were for the most part surplus World War I artillery adapted for coast defense purposes. At the outbreak of World War II, these weapons were deployed temporarily to cover harbors with inadequate defenses, until permanent works were constructed. Cape Henlopen, DE, and Cay May, NJ, at the mouth of Delaware Bay were two such sites. To quickly provide protection to this important shipping route, the army sent several coast artillery units equipped with 8in. railway guns and mobile 155 guns. Seen here are four 8in. MkVI Mod3A2 navy guns on army M1A1 railway mounts in firing position. Sand revetments, which still exist, protected each railway gun and crew. The concrete fire control tower (left) provided range and azimuth data to the railway battery. The maximum range for these guns was about 18 miles. This is Battery 21 at Fort Miles, Cape Henlopen, part of the Harbor Defenses of the Delaware, in early 1943. The battery site today is open to the public as part of Cape Henlopen State Park.

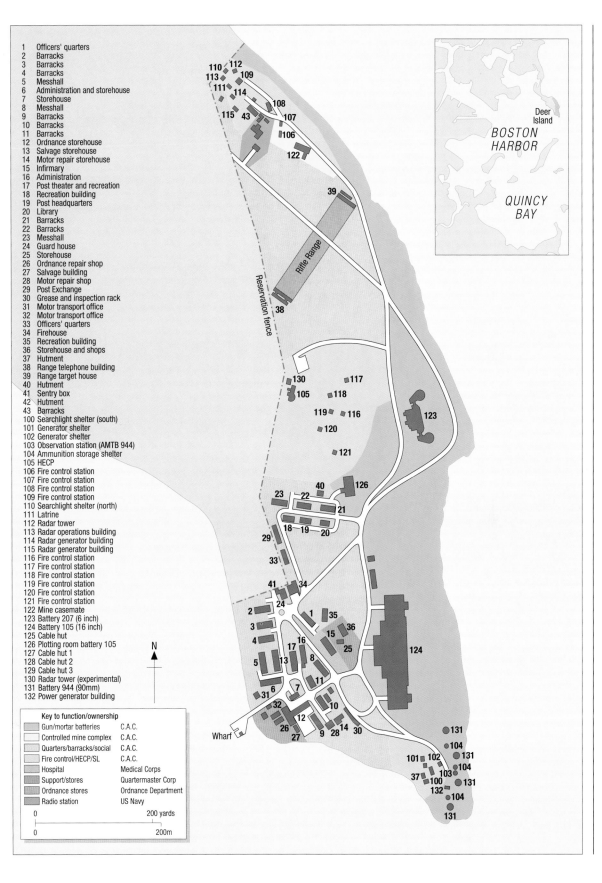

1 Officers' quarters
2 Barracks
3 Barracks
4 Barracks
5 Messhall
6 Administration and storehouse
7 Storehouse
8 Messhall
9 Barracks
10 Barracks
11 Barracks
12 Ordnance storehouse
13 Salvage storehouse
14 Motor repair storehouse
15 Infirmary
16 Administration
17 Post theater and recreation
18 Recreation building
19 Post headquarters
20 Library
21 Barracks
22 Barracks
23 Messhall
24 Guard house
25 Storehouse
26 Ordnance repair shop
27 Salvage building
28 Motor repair shop
29 Post Exchange
30 Grease and inspection rack
31 Motor transport office
32 Motor transport office
33 Officers' quarters
34 Firehouse
35 Recreation building
36 Storehouse and shops
37 Hutment
38 Range telephone building
39 Range target house
40 Hutment
41 Sentry box
42 Hutment
43 Barracks
100 Searchlight shelter (south)
101 Generator shelter
102 Generator shelter
103 Observation station (AMTB 944)
104 Ammunition storage shelter
105 HECP
106 Fire control station
107 Fire control station
108 Fire control station
109 Fire control station
110 Searchlight shelter (north)
111 Latrine
112 Radar tower
113 Radar operations building
114 Radar generator building
115 Radar generator building
116 Fire control station
117 Fire control station
118 Fire control station
119 Fire control station
120 Fire control station
121 Fire control station
122 Mine casemate
123 Battery 207 (6 inch)
124 Battery 105 (16 inch)
125 Cable hut
126 Plotting room battery 105
127 Cable hut 1
128 Cable hut 2
129 Cable hut 3
130 Radar tower (experimental)
131 Battery 944 (90mm)
132 Power generator building

Key to function/ownership

Gun/mortar batteries	C.A.C.
Controlled mine complex	C.A.C.
Quarters/barracks/social	C.A.C.
Fire control/HECP/SL	C.A.C.
Hospital	Medical Corps
Support/stores	Quartermaster Corp
Ordnance stores	Ordnance Department
Radio station	US Navy

0   200 yards
0   200m

Deer Island

BOSTON HARBOR

QUINCY BAY

N

Reservation fence

Rifle Range

Wharf

ABOVE Official quartermaster photo of Building 10, an Endicott-Taft barracks at Fort Michie, on Great Gull Island, NY, in Long Island Sound. (NARA Textual)

expanded from a few key buildings to include virtually the entire fort.

Transportation was a major quartermaster responsibility. The isolation of most seacoast forts meant most men and supplies were transported by water. The quartermasters supplied the ships and also built and maintained the wharves, a considerable expense where they were exposed to storms.

Permanent structures

Most of the non-tactical structures at the forts constructed during the Endicott-Taft period were designed to be permanent. Wood-frame buildings, sided with brick, clapboard, or stucco, were built on stone foundations, with slate roofs. The Quartermaster Corps designed standard plans for all types of non-tactical buildings. Those designed at the turn of the century, when most coast defense forts were constructed, were Colonial Revival, with elements of Queen Anne style in the officers' quarters. As the century progressed, new styles were adopted, such as Italianate and Spanish Revival and these styles were used when additional buildings were constructed. Storehouses and utilities were simpler and more utilitarian.

The building interiors were finished with wood floors, plaster walls with wood trim, and pressed metal ceilings. Structures where officers and men lived or worked had electricity, running water, and flush toilets, although some posts had long waits for these amenities. Single barracks housed a company of artillerymen, while double barracks were two barracks built end-to-end. Harbor defense headquarters posts often had a band barracks.

Officer's quarters varied in size and elaborateness depending upon the rank of the officer. The commanding officer occupied the largest and most elaborate of the officers' quarters, while other senior officers lived in single quarters and the majority of the quarters were duplexes for two families. Large forts had a bachelor officers' quarters with its separate mess. NCO quarters were usually double sets.

Virtually every post had a hospital, especially the more isolated posts. During World War II, with improved transportation, the trend was toward dispensaries at smaller posts, with hospitals at the larger posts.

The army took recreation seriously by the turn of the century, not only to maintain physical fitness and provide wholesome activities for off-duty soldiers, but also to promote a competitiveness that prepared men for combat. Although the soldiers used the parade ground as a general athletic field, facilities for tennis, handball, and baseball were also built in open areas, sometimes by volunteer troop labor. Large forts also featured a gymnasium and bowling alley.

Maintenance, supply, and transportation required numerous buildings. Carpenter and plumbing shops, quartermaster and commissary storehouses, ordnance storehouses and work shop (usually at the harbor defense headquarters post), stables and wagon sheds, power and pumping plants, coal storage, and wood sheds were usually all located in the same area, often near the quartermaster wharf.

Cantonments and temporary non-tactical buildings

In addition to the permanent structures, many temporary buildings were constructed, usually in response to temporary wartime expansion. While the army's initial response was frequently to house troops in tents, even in Alaska, the army made every effort to provide better shelter as rapidly as possible. Wood-framed and sided structures were built on posts or frost walls, rather than permanent foundations, but most were constructed according to standard plans.

During World War I, the Quartermaster Corps created standardized "600-series" temporary wooden buildings that could be quickly and inexpensively constructed all over the country. When America began to gear up for possible involvement in World War II and the peacetime draft was instituted, the Quartermaster Corps created new standardized designs of temporary "mobilization" buildings for a new generation of camps. The 700- and 800-series buildings – over 300 different types – were more elaborate and better built than the 600-series. Although only designed to last five to twenty-five years, these structures reflected America's heightened level of expectations, with wood framing 36in. on center, drop-wood siding, rolled asphalt roofing, double-hung windows, central heating, and running water. Large numbers of these buildings were constructed at permanent coastal forts in 1940 and 1941, as the 700-series gave way to the even more substantial 800-series. These sturdy structures housed the men of the National Guard called to active duty in the fall of 1940 and the draftees that expanded the CAC thereafter.

If land were available, the buildings were in groups that served individual batteries of men: several barracks, a mess hall, a recreation building, and a battery administration-storehouse building. If land was scarce, buildings went wherever space was available. On December 1, 1941, the Corps of Engineers took over building non-tactical structures from the Quartermaster Corps.

World War II coast artillery forts and reservations

As the United States entered World War II, temporary non-tactical structures adopted for war zones were modified and improved for use in the United States. "Modified theater-of-operations," or MTO, buildings were truly temporary, with wood framing 48in. on center, fiberboard sheathing, and 15 lb. rolled felt siding held on with wooden battens. Like the World War I designs, they had separate barracks and latrines, heated by magazine stoves or space heaters. In 1942, the US War Department ordered MTO buildings built at all new posts, and for the expansion of existing camps, posts, and stations. Fortunately, since most coastal forts already had mobilization-style buildings, fewer harbor defense units were quartered in MTO buildings.

The MTO designs were subject to continual change, for efficiency of construction, to minimize use of critical materials, and to improve their habitability. Designs combined features of the 700-series with theater-of-operations designs, and included additional bracing, improved insulation and ventilation, and a variety of sidings other than tarpaper.

MTO buildings vanished almost immediately after the war, but a number of mobilization-style buildings remain. Meanwhile, many permanent buildings are gone, casualties of limited maintenance budgets. However, the few forts that do include a wide range of non-tactical buildings give a strikingly different view of what active coastal forts really looked like.

BELOW General plan and section for BCN 213 at Fort Burnside, RI. These Corps of Engineers drawings show the layout for a 200-Series 6in. shielded BC battery in this, as of September 1944. (NARA Textual, RG 77, Entry 1007)

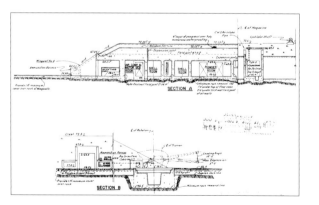

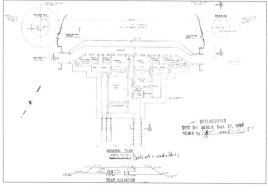

Armament and batteries

Endicott-Taft mortar and gun design

The United States moved into the breech-loading era conservatively, modifying earlier practice as little as possible. However, years of experimentation had finally established steel as the essential material, at least for high-powered guns, and faced with a choice, the army's Ordnance Department chose the French Debange screw breech with obturator over the German Krupp sliding breech.

There was considerable interchangeability between guns and carriages, with several different models of guns fitting one carriage and more than one model of carriage taking a given model of gun. While batteries were built for specific carriages, the differences were often minor, and not beyond alteration.

Endicott-Taft battery design

Endicott-Taft gun and mortar batteries presented a schizophrenic image. From the rear, they were impressive concrete structures, with doors, windows, and stairs, surmounted by large guns and carriages. From the front, the only thing visible was a mass of sodded earth or sand. From above, they showed their full extent, with guns in the middle of wide expanses of concrete. The concrete, however, was somewhat misleading. Like the earthen batteries built during the 1870s, the new batteries primarily relied on earth or sand for protection. While early batteries had thick concrete walls, the thickness of the vertical concrete was reduced, since three feet of sand was cheaper than one foot of concrete, and equally effective.

Battery design evolved considerably over 25 years. The engineers built the first batteries without practical tests, modifying earlier designs as little as possible. As they gained practical experience, they modified and improved their designs, enlarging magazines and improving waterproofing and ventilation. Some devices were retained, such as voice tubes; despite the general adoption of the telephone, the army continued to build and use them. Obsolete devices were omitted and new equipment installed, while redundant systems were provided for key functions. Meanwhile, older batteries were modified at considerable expense and effort, although a few whose design or location did not justify their maintenance were abandoned.

Spanish-American War emergency batteries

Before the rearmament sparked by the Endicott Report had progressed very far, the country went to war with Spain, and an exaggerated fear of the Spanish fleet

BOTTOM LEFT M1888 12in. gun on BC M1892 at Battery Godfrey, Fort Scott, CA, in 1909. This early Endicott-Taft battery was constructed in 1895 for a large-caliber gun on barbette carriage. Note the shell cart and crane on the gun carriage to move the projectile to the breech. (US Army Casemate Museum)

BOTTOM RIGHT M1895 12in. gun on DC M1896 at Battery DeRussey, Fort Monroe, VA, in 1912. At the moment of firing, this gun is in the raised position on a Buffington-Crozier disappearing carriage, the most common Endicott-Taft carriage. (US Army Casemate Museum)

swept the Atlantic and Gulf seaboards. Innumerable coastal towns and cities frantically petitioned their elected representatives for protection.

The army, not immune to political pressure, attempted to mollify the populace without diverting material needed for the invasion of Cuba. As appropriations for seacoast defenses soared, contractors' crews worked multiple shifts to complete new batteries. Lower-priority locations received emergency batteries of large muzzle-loading Rodman guns or breech-loading siege guns and howitzers, but the siege pieces were soon withdrawn to equip the army going to Cuba; some were replaced by antique US Civil War field guns.

Because large gun barrels and breeches were harder and more time consuming to fabricate than their carriages, the army had acquired more modern guns than carriages. In the crisis, the Ordnance Department decided as a stopgap to modify old carriages built for 15in. Rodman guns, altering them to take the new 8in. breech-loading guns. Twenty-one were to be emplaced in simple batteries, but few if any were ready before the end of the brief war and some were never completed. The guns were soon dismounted, and most were eventually mounted on modern carriages. While many of the emplacements were strictly temporary, with sand-covered timber magazines, a few were substantial concrete emplacements, with concrete magazines.

ABOVE M1890 12in. BLM on MC M1896MI at Battery Anderson, Fort Monroe, VA, in 1918. The first primary weapon developed during the Endicott-Taft System was the mortar to take advantage of the thin deck armor of contemporary warships. (US Army Casemate Museum)

Breech-loading mortars, carriages, and batteries

The first modern weapon to be completed was the 12in. M1886 breech-loading mortar (BLM). The only modern cannon that could be made of cast iron, because of their low velocity and chamber pressure, they were mounted on the M1891 mortar carriage (MC). The M1886 BLM soon gave way to the steel M1890 BLM on the M1896 MC, increasing the range. The last few batteries were built for longer, more powerful mortars or more efficient carriages, but never both.

The first mortar batteries were based on an experimental battery for muzzle-loading mortars built by Col. Henry Abbott at Willets Point, NY. This "Abbott quad" was in the form of a rectangle, with one 4-mortar pit in each corner. While designed to maximize the effectiveness of the mortars, experience revealed that the blast effect of short weapons in confined pits was excessive, so subsequent battery designs placed the pits in line, with open backs. Most batteries were four-pit, but some batteries had only two pits for eight mortars, and one single-pit battery was built. Before World War I, experience showed that four mortars were too many to serve efficiently in one pit, so two mortars were removed from most pits.

BELOW Battery Worth, Fort Pickens, Santa Rosa Island, FL, from 500ft in 1994. This battery was built in 1899 for eight mortars. In 1918, four of its mortars were removed, while the other four remained until 1942. In 1943, this battery became the location of the HECP-HDCP for HD of Pensacola. The large building in the center of the battery was built for that purpose. (McGovern Collection)

Large- and intermediate-caliber gun and carriage design

Guns, with greater chamber pressure and heavier recoil, were not ready for service until after the mortars. All were steel, built up by shrinking a series of hoops on a rifled tube. The first generation, the M1888, was produced in three sizes: 8, 10, and 12in. The 8in. gun, ready for service first, was already outclassed by guns afloat, and only one model of that size was produced. The 10 and 12in. guns soon followed. In 1895, an improved breech mechanism replaced two cranks with one, and in 1900, larger chambers increased muzzle velocity, but excessive bore erosion forced a reduction in the velocity.

These guns were mounted on both barbette (BC) and disappearing carriages (DC). The barbette carriages were developed first, using the Vavasseur design, in which the upper carriage recoiled back and up an inclined slope, similar to the carriages used for the older Rodman muzzle-loaders. Standard barbette carriages for all three gun sizes were produced, but these early barbette carriages were obsolescent, and production was soon discontinued as the disappearing carriage proved successful.

The Buffington-Crozier disappearing carriage was a revolutionary American design that came to characterize the Endicott-Taft System. When the gun fired, the top carriage with the gun recoiled back, and heavy arms lowered the gun behind the thick parapet while raising a massive counterweight. This not only protected the weapon and its crew, and hid them from sight; it lowered the breech of the gun so that it could be reloaded without having to hoist the heavy shells. While increasingly complicated, and not without their detractors, over 400 Buffington-Crozier disappearing carriages were manufactured, for guns from six to sixteen inches. When naval guns began to fire at higher elevations and longer ranges, the protection offered by the parapet became less important. Their biggest disadvantage was their restricted range due to their limited elevation. Although the last 16in. model was capable of 30 degrees and 14in. carriages could manage 20 degrees, the smaller carriages, even when modified, could not exceed 15 degrees. As the elevation and range of naval guns increased, this became increasingly critical. By the end of World War I, the disappearing carriage was only recommended for sites where rapidity of fire was more important than long range.

Ninety-two 8in. guns (9 barbette and 64 disappearing carriages), one hundred sixty-four 10in. guns (11 barbette and 128 disappearing carriages), and one hundred sixty-one 12in. guns (33 barbette and 83 disappearing carriages) were produced. More guns than carriages were manufactured to allow for spare tubes.

After the turn of the century, increasing battleship armor threatened to make existing seacoast guns obsolete, especially as the increased range of naval guns meant they could strike from farther away. Since the muzzle velocity of the 12in. gun could not be increased without prohibitive bore erosion, the solution adopted was the 14in. gun, firing a 1,660 lb. projectile at a lower

Hoists

Most Endicott-Taft batteries were on two levels, with the guns on the upper level and ammunition on the lower. Some mechanical device was necessary to move projectiles that could weigh well over 1,000 lb. up to the gun level. The first method, block and tackle suspended from a crane at the back of the platform, was far too slow.

Next to be widely adopted was the balanced-platform hoist. Pairs of boxes, like elevator cars, were connected by cables, so when one was at the proper level on the lower story, the other was at the correct height at the upper story. An empty shot cart was rolled on the upper car as a full one was rolled onto the lower car. Raising the lower car lowered the upper one. However, it proved impossible to keep the cars positioned correctly as the cables stretched.

Next was the Hodges hoist, two flat-link chains in continuous loops between two sets of sprockets on axles, one axle on each level. A hand crank or electric motor turned the lower axle, causing the chain to lift the projectile in cup-shaped arms to the upper delivery table. These chain hoists worked for 6in. and 8in. projectiles, but less well for larger ones.

The Taylor-Raymond hoist used chains like the Hodges hoist, but with carriers of a different design. The Taylor-Raymond hoist was efficient and reliable, with numerous electrical safety features. Almost all large-caliber batteries were either built with Taylor-Raymond hoists, or were modified to accept them. Later batteries were built with magazines on the same level, eliminating the need for ammunition hoists. The accompanying photo to the right shows Taylor-Raymond ammunition hoist, Battery Warwick, Fort Wint, Subic Bay, PI, June 3, 1909 (NARA Still Pictures No. 77-F-111-78-16).

velocity, giving increased power while keeping bore erosion within manageable limits. Of the 27 made, four were mounted in army-designed turrets on unique Fort Drum, the "concrete battleship" in Manila Bay. All the rest went on disappearing carriages: four in Los Angeles, the rest overseas in Panama, Oahu, and the Philippines.

The 6in. gun was an intermediate caliber, the smallest to use a disappearing carriage. At the same time, its 100 lb. projectile was the largest that could be carried by hand. It had characteristics of both larger and smaller calibers, and some were employed like major-caliber armament, with appropriate fire control, while others were used as rapid-fire guns to protect mine fields and to defend against torpedo boats. Heavier guns having priority, the first 6in. gun was the M1897. The primary difference between subsequent models was the style of breechblock, although the ill-fated experiment with high-velocity M1900 guns was repeated in this caliber. The last model, the M1908 gun, was a radical departure. Wire-wound instead of built-up, it was half the weight of a built-up gun.

The 6in. barbette carriages were a very different design from the older, larger ones. These pedestal mounts, much more modern, carried the gun in a cradle, with concentric recoil. The carriage and crew were given limited protection by a thick shield. The disappearing carriages generally resembled those of the larger guns. Two hundred eight 6in. guns (51 barbette and 152 disappearing carriages) were produced.

Endicott-Taft gun battery designs

Major-caliber Endicott-Taft gun batteries also evolved, if not as markedly as mortar batteries. In general, they maintained the same appearance – as many as four wide emplacements, but usually two, separated by concrete traverse magazines that both stored ammunition and protected against enfilade fire. The primary changes were in the details.

The first change was enlarging the magazines, a need recognized almost immediately. At this time, the batteries were two-story, and artillerymen hoisted projectiles up to the guns by block and tackle, using simple davits. When these proved unable to supply ammunition as rapidly as the guns could fire, several types of ammunition hoists were tried, culminating in the Taylor-Raymond chain hoist, which was retrofitted into most of the earlier large-caliber batteries. It was a complex device, driven by a large electric motor, but it supplied ammunition as fast as the guns could fire. A simpler design used in the 6in. batteries, the Hodges hoist, relied on hand power. Powder hoists were also widely installed, but in the end were abandoned in favor of carrying the powder bags by hand through the use of handbarrows.

FOLLOWING PAGE **Abbott-quad mortar battery**
Mortar batteries were a primary weapon system of the Endicott-Taft System. Started in 1890, Battery McCook-Reynolds, Fort Hancock, Sandy Hook, NJ, in the defenses of New York, represents the first design, which placed sixteen 12in. mortars in four square pits. When all 16 mortars were fired at once, a shotgun-like pattern descended on the thin deck armor of the warship of that period. This design was later abandoned due to the muzzle blast in the confined space. Fort Hancock's only mortar battery is seen here from a tethered balloon used for fire control. The balloon observer is looking down from his basket at the battery with its unique ditch, counterscarp wall, and machine-gun galleries. An outline of its underground galleries and magazines can be seen. One mortar was removed from each pit in 1917 to arm a battery on the Navesink Highlands, on the mainland behind Sandy Hook. This view dates from 1918, the year before the mortar battery was decommissioned. In 1920, its remaining M1886 cast-iron mortars on M1891 carriages were removed and scrapped. During World War II, the structure housed the harbor defense command post. Battery McCook-Reynolds today is open to the public as part of the Gateway NRA, NPS.

Electricity

The first Endicott-Taft batteries did not need electricity. They had no motors, and kerosene lanterns supplied light. Soon, however, electricity was necessary for ammunition hoists, as well as the motors now on gun carriages. Although civilians were beginning to adopt alternating current, the army required direct current for both motors and searchlights. Because it was too expensive to operate steam power plants continuously, and due to the long time required to build up steam, steam plants were used to periodically charge storage batteries, which supplied power for short periods.

Steam plants, however, were complex and required skilled operators, so the army eventually turned to gasoline power. In 1910, the army adopted a gasoline engine direct coupled to a 25 kW generator, cooled by a radiator with an electric fan. These sets were highly successful, and were used in every coastal fort, not only for the batteries, but also for searchlights and other tactical installations.

The engineers insisted on redundancy for the essential power. Where two motor-generators were needed, three were provided, so the battery could still operate while one was being serviced. As commercial power became more common and less expensive, batteries were commonly connected to the commercial electric power grid, with emplacement power plants serving as backup.

With the coming of World War II, diesel engines were adopted for the new generation of batteries, but the old gasoline engines continued to serve to the war's end.

Abbott-quad mortar battery

Disappearing gun battery

Large-caliber breech-loading guns on "disappearing carriages" were the signature weapons of the Endicott-Taft System. Started in 1898, Battery Pensacola, Fort Pickens, Santa Rosa Island, FL, in the defenses of Pensacola, was built inside a Third System fort. It mounted two M1895 12in. guns on M1897 disappearing carriages in a large two-story concrete emplacement. This 1918 view shows the upper level with the loading platforms and the guns, while the lower level contained magazines, plotting room and storage rooms. The battery commander's station projects above the top of the battery. The battery today is open to the public as part of Gulf Island NSS, NPS.

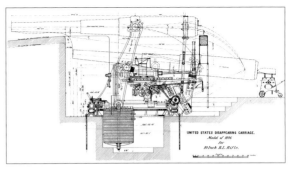

ABOVE Two M1895 12in. guns on DC M1896 and BC M1892 at Battery Huger, Fort Sumter, SC, in April 1921. This combination of barbette and disappearing carriage in one battery was most unusual. Note how most of this famous Third System fort has been leveled to make way for the Endicott-Taft battery. (NARA Still Pictures No. 38-FCD-99)

TOP LEFT M1895M1 12in. gun on BCLR M1917 at Battery Kingman #1, Fort Hancock, Sandy Hook, NJ, in June 1919. Firing practice is under way at Battery Kingman. The M1917 carriage allowed for a maximum elevation of 35 degrees, which added about 10,000 yds to the range of these 12in. guns as compared to the same gun mounted on a disappearing carriage. (NARA Still Pictures SC-60720)

TOP RIGHT Plan for an M1896 10in. gun on a DC M1896 in an emplacement. The Buffington-Crozier disappearing carriage raised the gun to fire over the parapet by use of a counterweight. The gun recoiled back down into the emplacement to be reloaded, protected from direct fire. (NARA Cartographic No. 165-113-1)

The first batteries were lit by kerosene lanterns – sometimes well into the 20th century. Those early batteries that did have electricity were often equipped with storage batteries, charged from steam-powered power plants. In 1910, the army adopted the gasoline engine, and 25kW motor-generators became standard for larger batteries, in addition to such auxiliaries as searchlights. As commercial power became more common, the artillery came to rely on it, retaining the battery power plant as a backup.

For years, the batteries were plagued by dampness, injurious to both ammunition and electrical equipment. The engineers learned to design batteries with air passages and ventilation, while modifying older batteries to decrease and control the moisture. In addition, experience had shown that the loading platform, the concrete surface surrounding the gun, did not allow enough room to efficiently ram the projectiles and powder. Over several years, the engineers enlarged almost every platform, with the coincidental benefit of increasing the storage space below.

Originally, the magazines were below the level of the gun and loading platform, so the thick overhead cover of the traverse would not project above the horizontal crest of the battery and give away the position. The battery commander was to be with his plotting room, below the primary fire-control station, away from the battery. After the battery commanders complained, their stations were moved to the batteries, followed by the plotting rooms. The stations, however, projected above the crest of the battery, spoiling the concealment. Since there was now no reason to keep the traverses low, the magazines were raised to the level of the gun platform, eliminating the need for ammunition hoists. Projectiles could then be loaded on carts and pushed directly to the guns.

These changes were not rapid, and since years could pass between design and completion of a battery, the chronology was not exact, but the progression was clear. Engineers kept abreast of progress at other sites, and of the success or failure of experiments, so that new batteries could be designed with the most modern features. At the same time, older batteries were modified as much as possible, with such features as ammunition hoists, wider platforms, power plants, and even latrines. The engineers learned as they built, applying what they learned not only to the batteries they were building, but also to those already built.

The final large-caliber Endicott-Taft batteries were for 14in. guns, one twin-gun battery on Oahu, four single-gun batteries in Manila Bay, six batteries in Panama for ten guns, and two twin-gun batteries at Los Angeles, subsequently split into single-gun batteries for tactical purposes. These disappearing batteries embodied everything the engineers had learned, and were models of efficiency and simplicity. Only the battery on Oahu and one in the Philippines employed ammunition hoists, while none of the later Panama batteries did. Unlike the Philippine batteries, the traverses of the Panama batteries were designed with sloping sidewalls of sand, rather than vertical concrete, increasing the distance between the guns. The Los Angeles batteries (actually begun in 1916 but their guns and carriages more properly fall into the Endicott-Taft System) followed the general design of the two single-gun 14in. batteries at Fort Sherman in the Panama Canal Zone.

Rapid-fire guns, carriages, and batteries

When adopted, the 5in. gun was believed to be the largest whose projectile could be carried by hand, an assumption soon found to be false. Similar to the corresponding models of 6in. gun, the 5in. gun fired a projectile of almost 60 lb. All 5in. guns were on two models of barbette carriage. The 1896 carriage for the M1897 gun was a balanced pillar design. Mounted on a tall cylinder, it was cranked down, out of sight, and only raised for action. Unlike the disappearing carriage, it did not descend after each shot. A relatively thin shield offered some protection to the gun and crew. The M1903 carriage for the M1900 gun was a standard pedestal mount, resembling those for the 6in. gun, including the smaller, thicker shield. Only fifty-three 5in. coast defense guns were manufactured.

The United States found itself going to war with Spain without any effective defense against torpedo boats. As a stopgap, thirty-four 4.72in. and eight 6in. British Armstrong guns on central pivot (pedestal) mounts were purchased abroad, some arriving before and some after the war. Unlike any of the domestic weapons, they were always odd man out.

The primary defense against torpedo boats and protection for mine fields was the 3in. gun, often referred to as the 15-pdr, from the nominal weight of its projectile. The first model, the M1898, was on a "masking parapet" mount, a proprietary version of the balanced pillar. The next two models were Bethlehem Steel's M1902 and the Ordnance Department's M1903, both on pedestal mounts with concentric recoil. As their designated targets increased in size, the 15 lb. projectiles were deemed too light, and by the time the defenses of the Panama Canal were constructed, they were replaced by 6in. guns. Two hundred eighty-seven 3in. guns were produced.

Rapid-fire batteries were simpler. Emplacements were rounded or square, depending on the field of fire, and parapets were low; shields provided the only protection. Since they employed fixed ammunition, only one magazine per gun was required. Ammunition was hand-carried from these rooms to the guns. Plotting rooms were seldom needed, and only one or two storerooms. Battery commanders' stations were not built with the batteries, but many were added later.

Atypical Endicott-Taft guns and batteries

Several unique or atypical batteries were constructed. The first Endicott-Taft gun battery was Battery Potter at Fort Hancock, a two-gun 12in. gun-lift battery. This unique structure protected the guns and crew during loading by lowering the guns, on their barbette carriages, by means of large platform lifts. The guns descended to the lower level for loading and rose for firing. Requiring a massive steam-powered hydraulic system, this battery design became instantly obsolete when the Buffington-Crozier disappearing carriage proved satisfactory. One M1895 16in. gun was built, a

ABOVE Two M1898 3in. guns on MP M1898 at Battery Irwin, Fort Monroe, VA, in April 1918. Firing practice is under way at this four-gun battery. The officer in the battery commander's station is operating an M1910 azimuth instrument to spot the fall of the shells. Note the 6-pdr RF guns in the background in front of the mine planter. (NARA Still Pictures 111-SC-9802)

BELOW Two M1897 5in. guns on BP M1896 at Battery McGrath, Fort Rosecrans, CA. Only 16 emplacements for 5in. guns on balanced-pillar mounts were constructed during the Endicott-Taft System. The carriage lowered the gun below the parapet when not in use, but this arrangement was found to be unstable. (US Army Casemate Museum)

ABOVE Battery Potter, Fort Hancock, NJ, from 500ft in 1997. This large three-story concrete and stone structure contained two 12in. guns on platforms, as well as ammunition magazines and steam plant for the lifting machinery. The high cost, slow rate of fire, and mechanical complexity made this the first and last gun-lift battery. By 1907, the battery was decommissioned and a group of fire-control stations replaced its guns. (McGovern Collection)

combination of an experiment, learning tool, and public relations centerpiece. After the gun sat for some years at the proving ground, a single disappearing carriage was built for it and a one-gun battery was constructed in Panama. While the design of the single-story battery was unique, this owed more to its location atop a steep hill than to the one-of-a-kind gun and carriage.

Two turrets for 14in. guns were set in the massive concrete structure of Fort Drum, in Manila Bay. While impressively impervious to hostile fire, even in 1942, the "concrete battleship" was a maintenance headache, and the turrets' restricted elevation limited their range. Many of the batteries in the defenses of the Delaware River were unusual, and the most so were two 3in. guns installed in casemates made from old powder magazines at Fort Mott. None of these unusual designs was exactly a failure, but none was repeated, due to cost or complexity.

Even farther afield, Congress forced the army to buy and emplace several strange-looking pneumatic guns. Called "Zalinski dynamite guns" for the artillery officer who developed, or at least marketed them, they mostly resembled large sewer pipes. The concept was simple – compressed air could launch high explosives without risk of explosion, at a time when guns could only fire projectiles with black powder charges. In practice, the range of the pneumatic guns was limited, while they required a steam plant, compressors, and piping. When the Ordnance Department soon solved the problem of firing high explosives from normal guns, the dynamite gun was quickly abandoned.

Post World War I guns, carriages, and batteries

The next era coincided with World War I, although the length of time to design and construct a fortification system meant it was not strictly a wartime measure. By 1915, battleships could outrange coast defense guns on disappearing carriages, and attempts to redesign the carriages for higher elevation were less than successful. All the same, the increased range and elevation of naval gunfire meant disappearing carriages no longer offered the same protection they once did. The United States did have a number of perfectly adequate spare M1895 12in. gun barrels for which there was no pressing need. While development of a 16in. gun and carriage was proceeding, in the short term a new barbette carriage that would allow the existing 12in. barrels to fire at elevations up to 35 degrees would be both powerful and economical.

The resulting battery design resembled the last generation of 14in. batteries, begun the same year to defend the new port at Los Angeles. The primary difference was the substitution of barbette carriages for disappearing ones. The new batteries, first begun in 1916, were largely constructed within the next five years. The carriages, necessarily emplaced in large, round, open emplacements, had no real parapet to protect men or guns. The central traverse magazine, a concrete structure covered with earth, contained the ammunition, a small power plant, and two plotting rooms, so each gun could track separate targets and send firing data to the guns by long rods through tunnels to a mechanical range indicator within view of the gun crew.

Fifteen 2-gun batteries were built, generally similar except for Fort Mills, on Corregidor Island in Manila Bay, where the two emplacements were some distance apart. Originally considered one battery, it was eventually designated as two.

Seacoast ammunition

All the effort to build seacoast guns and erect batteries was wasted without reliable and effective ammunition. Seacoast artillery ammunition was composed of four basic elements. A primer at the base of the charge ignited the propellant in the gun. This explosion forced the projectile out of the gun, and the fuze detonated the explosive charge when the projectile struck.

Smaller pieces – 37mm, 40mm, 3in., and 90mm guns – used fixed ammunition, joining the projectile with the propellant in a metal case resembling a large rifle cartridge, with a primer in its base. In the smaller calibers, these were quick to load and helped seal the breech.

Five-inch and larger guns were separately loaded. First the projectile and then the powder were rammed into the breech, the powder in a raw silk bag, tightly laced to the proper diameter. Propellant in the 19th century was brown prismatic powder, a form of gunpowder. Smokeless powder replaced this just after the turn of the century. After closing the breechblock, a primer was inserted.

Service projectiles were mostly hardened steel armor-piercing (AP) shot or shell, with base fuzes. Shot had a thicker case and smaller explosive charge than shell. High explosive (HE) projectiles contained the maximum explosive charge, to attack the unarmored portion of ships. Black powder was an unsatisfactory explosive charge; after the turn of the century, it was replaced by high explosives, primarily "explosive D" (ammonium picrate). Beginning around 1905, the points of AP projectiles were covered by small caps of softer metal, to improve their armor penetration. By 1910, new projectiles were longer, and fitted with thin metal ballistic windshields. The improved aerodynamic shape significantly increased the range. Target-practice projectiles were cast iron, much cheaper than steel, while dummy projectiles were used only for loading drills.

HE bursting charges required effective fuzes, which had to remain inert when the gun was fired and yet detonate reliably after the projectile had passed through thick armor plating. The Ordnance Department led the world in this field, producing effective fuzes as early as 1902.

Mortars differed somewhat from this pattern. Most importantly, they used zone powder charges, a series of incremental charges that increased the range in steps, while the elevation was varied between 45 and 65 degrees to produce a specific range. Some mortar projectiles, while generally similar to those for the guns, had different names, such as deck-piercing and torpedo shell (HE). Mortars also had different driving bands (copper gas seals), due to their lower muzzle velocity.

The nominal weight of a 12in. projectile was 1,000 lb. for a gun or mortar; a cap and windshield increased this to 1,070 lb. Both 12in. guns and mortars, however, also had lighter projectiles for increased range.

Seacoast ammunition, designed to attack ships, generally required projectiles with strong cases and small explosive charges. The fuzes were base-mounted, with a delay to allow the projectile to pass through armor. These features, however, made normal seacoast projectiles ill suited for use against land targets. Attempts to supply coast artillery forts with projectiles for use against land targets were largely unavailing, but on Corregidor in 1942, fuzes were altered to eliminate the delay, enhancing their effect against land targets.

BELOW A 12in. shot cart at Battery Kingman, Fort Hancock, Sandy Hook, NJ on June 24, 1919. This cart is designed to bring the 12in. shell from the loading tables in the magazine out to the breech of the gun on the open emplacement. The gun crew would then use a ramrod to seat the shell into the breech. (NARA Still Pictures SC-60717)

US Army controlled submarine mines

BELOW Preparations are under way at the mine wharf to load mines, cables, and anchors onto US Army mine planter *General Ord.* (NARA Still Pictures SC-91555)

Submarine mines, originally called "torpedoes," had a long history in America. During the Civil War, mines were an important and effective part of Confederate river and harbor defense. They were, however, largely uncontrolled; once laid they were dangerous to any passing vessel, friendly or unfriendly.

One key lesson of the Civil War was that ironclads, if not stopped by obstructions, could pass strong batteries without fatal damage. Submarine mines could obstruct those channels, and in 1865 the Board of Engineers recommended the use of mines for harbor defense. In 1869, the development of a modern submarine mining system was assigned to Col. Henry L. Abbot, commandant of the Engineer School at Willets Point, NY. Over the next 20 years, Abbot labored to perfect submarine mines, and his basic system, with revised and updated mechanical and electrical equipment, was used through World War II. Meanwhile, in 1886 the Endicott Report again called for submarine mines.

Submarine mines were a vital aspect of harbor defense, particularly at night and other times of reduced visibility. They could attack enemy ships even when the ships could not be clearly seen, and even when visibility was good, they forced the ships to slow or stop under fire of the guns. Their proven ability to intimidate naval commanders was also well documented. Later, their ability to detect and destroy submarines became paramount.

Controlled mines, with all essential items required to plant and operate them, were to be stored locally, in readiness for immediate use. In practice, however, most harbor defenses did not have on hand everything needed to plant the approved mine fields.

The army began installing mine defenses in major harbors during the 1880s. However, to avoid damage and deterioration, not to mention danger to friendly shipping, the mines themselves were not planted during peacetime. They were first deployed in 1898, during the Spanish-American War. The lessons learned then resulted in improvements in mine planting facilities, and what may be considered a standard system emerged. This was strictly an army operation; soldiers or army civilian employees, using army ships, planted the mines, which were then operated by soldiers.

OPPOSITE PAGE **Controlled mines**
This weapon system required a mine support complex on land and several types of vessels on the water. The complex shown here was built at Fort Wetherill, RI, on the rocky coast of the East Passage into Narragansett Bay. The support complex allowed the US Army mine planter *General Absalom Baird* to load mines, cables, mooring lines, anchors, and other gear. Also tied up to the wharf were distribution box boats (L-boats) and motor mine yawls (M-boats). A narrow-gauge tramway led off the mine wharf to the mine-loading room, where explosives were loaded into mine casings. The explosives were stored in a separate building behind the cable tank. The tramway also connected with the cable tank building, where reels of submarine cable were stored underwater, and to the mine storehouse where the mine casings, anchors, and other equipment were stored. Located behind the mine storehouse was the mine casemate, where the submarine cables rise out of the cable gallery from the seabed. These cables were connected to a large switchboard. The mines were controlled from the casemate, but since there was no view of the minefield from this location, the double mine station on the bluff above provided information to the mine plotting room located below them in the same building, which then relayed firing commands to the casemate. The mine complex has been converted into the Rhode Island Aquatic Research Facility.

Controlled mines

ABOVE Inside the mine casemate at Fort Wint, Subic Bay, PI, in April 1909. The board with large gauges controlled the electricity from the storage batteries, while each board with a knife switch controlled one mine. (NARA Still Pictures 77-F-111-121-26)

In 1901, the submarine mine program was transferred from the Corps of Engineers to the Artillery Corps, and by 1903, mine facilities were being constructed at many US harbors. The first four specially built mine planters were ordered in 1904, with four more in 1909, while mine facilities were also built in Panama, Hawaii, and the Philippines.

Some mine fields were laid during World War I, and in 1917, ten more mine planters were ordered. When the US Army Mine Planter Service was established in 1918, soldiers, supplemented by the local mine companies, replaced civilian mine planter crews. However, spending cuts in the 1920s eliminated all but five older mine planters and all but three new planters. This neglect continued into the 1930s.

In 1937 one new mine planter was ordered, and mine defenses were brought up to war footing with the construction of new facilities. In 1940, the army ordered 16 new planters to replace its aging fleet. New mines were designed and built, along with a few new facilities to maintain them. After the US entered World War II in 1941, mines were planted at major harbors around the continental United States and maintained throughout the war. During the war, responsibility for development and supply of mine *matériel* was transferred from the CAC to the Ordnance Department, and ground mines largely replaced buoyant mines. In 1944, some of the new mine planters were transferred to the navy. Between 1947 and 1949, all mine duties were transferred to the navy, who experimented with controlled harbor defense mines into the 1950s, before finally discontinuing them.

The mines

Submarine mines are controlled or uncontrolled, and buoyant or ground. Uncontrolled, or contact, mines, with no means to render them safe, can be detonated by any passing vessel, friendly or unfriendly. Controlled submarine mines are controlled from shore by an electrical connection. Commonly, the navy laid contact mines (note the terminology – the navy "laid" mines, the army "planted" them), closing selected channels to all vessels. The army planted controlled mines in a few main channels, where they could be observed from shore and protected by guns. At the same time, the navy operated other underwater defenses, such as nets and booms, and hydrophones, alongside army defenses.

Mines were composed of a casing, compound plug with mine transformer, fuzes, and circuit closer, moorings, and in the case of buoyant mines, anchors. They contained high explosive, such as dynamite, wet guncotton, or TNT, with TNT becoming standard after 1912. The circuit closer within the compound plug was the detection device, while the firing current acted through the transformer to fire the small fuzes, which in turn fired the primer that detonated the main explosive charge.

Buoyant mines floated, restrained by an anchor, high enough to be struck by a ship but deep enough to not be seen. In 1912, they could be used in water up to 150ft deep, while in 1942 this had increased to 300ft. However, the speed of the current limited this depth. They could not be used in water shallower than 20ft. The round steel cases contained the compound plug with its circuit closer, in addition to the explosive. Where increased buoyancy was needed due to the depth of water or force of the current, cylindrical sections, corrugated for strength, were added between the hemispherical halves of the case. The army planted both ground and buoyant mines in the Spanish-American War, but concentrated on buoyant mines until early 1943.

Ground mines were heavy cases that rested on the bottom. A buoy suspended above contained the circuit closer that triggered the mine. Due to the distance from the bottom of the ship, ground mines required larger explosive charges, but were less vulnerable to damage from currents and passing ships. Ground mines in 1912 contained 200–300 lb. of explosive, and were limited to water 35ft deep. The army planted some 4,000 controlled ground mines, each containing 3,000 lb. of explosive, between 1943 and 1945.

The circuit closer was triggered when a ship struck the case or buoy. Depending on the settings in the casemate, this either sent a signal to the casemate or exploded the mine. During World War II, magnetic and audio detectors could signal the casemate or trigger a mine when a ship or submarine passed close to them, even if not actually struck.

The controls in the mine casemate set the method of firing. In "contact fire," the mines detonated when struck. "Delayed-contact fire" allowed the vessel to pass more directly over the mine. In"observation (or command) fire," vessels were tracked from shore and when over a mine, the mine was fired by command. A mine set on "signal" lit a lamp in the casemate when a ship tripped the circuit closer. The commander could then fire the mine or order further investigation. Mines were set on "test" to confirm their electrical connections, and "off" to make them completely safe, such as when a convoy or naval vessel was entering or leaving port.

All the electricity for the mine system came from the casemate. The mines used direct current for operation, supervision, and signaling, but alternating current to fire a mine, a key safety feature.

Mine groups

Abbot's original grand group of mines consisted of seven groups, each of three mines 100ft apart, connected to a junction box. When fired by contact, only one mine exploded, but when fired by command, all three mines exploded. As cable with more conductors became available, the junction box was eliminated and the grand group consisted of 19 mines, each fired separately. Cables led from each mine to the distribution box, and a 19-conductor cable connected the distribution box to the casemate. In the 1930s, the 19-conductor cable was replaced with a single-conductor connecting stepping relays in the distribution box and casemate.

Mine groups were planted in straight lines, for ease of planting and maintenance. To cover a wide channel, groups were planted abreast. Normally, several lines of mines were employed, requiring many groups. During World War II, hydrophones and magnetic detectors were placed in advance of the first line of mines. The mine field was not normally planted outside the effective range of the rapid-fire guns. In 1912, this meant 4,500 yds; by 1942, it had been increased to 8,000 yds. Other factors were the location of supporting searchlights and insuring that a ship sunk by the mines did not block the channel.

After the war, when the navy assumed responsibility for harbor defense, they considered submarines, especially small ones, the most likely seaborne threat; so mines and their detection apparatus continued in service after the last guns had been silenced.

Mine buildings

An extensive assortment of structures supported the mine system. The mine (or torpedo) storehouse stored empty mines, anchors, compound plugs, circuit closers, shackles, mooring sockets, and other items. Movable overhead hoists used block and tackle to move heavy equipment. Explosives were stored in a magazine. Only a fraction of what was needed was kept at the post; an arsenal shipped the rest as needed. Fuzes were never stored with explosives. To prevent deterioration, large reels of heavy cable were stored underwater in cable tanks with overhead cranes, hoists, and tackle.

The mine components were brought from the storehouse, cable tanks, and magazines to the loading room, where they were assembled and tested by a detachment under the chief loader. Typically, the loading room was composed of two rooms, one for loading and assembling mines, the other for loading and assembling compound plugs. The loading room often had a small test tank and overhead hoist. Mines were loaded with explosives, fitted with their compound plugs, connected to their cables, tested for water tightness and circuit integrity, and then a complete group was assembled before being sent to the wharf.

A rail system connected all the mine facilities. If the post had a regular rail system, the tramway might have used the same gauge; if not, a 3ft-gauge system was usually installed. The men pushed the flat cars by hand unless a hill required a hoisting engine. The rail system ultimately led down to the mine wharf, a pier with a large work surface and a heavy loading derrick. Here the mines, cables, and distribution boxes would be loaded on the mine planter. Usually mine wharves had boathouses for storing smaller yawls and their equipment. Ideally, a post would have a separate wharf for mine activities, so as not to interfere with the mine planting, but often the mine wharf was used for other activities as well.

The mines used the same fire control as the big guns, with observing stations and mine commander's station. The plotting room, originally in the mine commander's station, was later moved to the casemate. The mines were controlled from the mine casemate, which held the firing controls. The 1890s mine casemates were in poorly ventilated underground concrete vaults. The moisture proved as detrimental to the equipment as the engine exhaust did to the personnel, so the next generation of casemates was built in the open, providing ventilation at the expense of protection. Finally, these casemates were enclosed in larger concrete rooms with bombproof covers, and new casemates were built of thick concrete, gasproofed with forced ventilation. The mine casemate, under the casemate electrician, was the heart of the system, with operating boards containing the master switches for the individual mines. The structure was divided into rooms for the operating board, generating equipment, storage batteries, and sleeping room. The electrical system included a direct-current generator, an 80-volt storage battery, a motor-generator to provide alternating current for firing, a casemate transformer, and a power panel to control the direct and alternating current.

Mine flotilla

The principal vessel of the mine flotilla was the mine planter, a large ship 160–200ft long. These were often not assigned to specific harbors, but traveled up and down the coast to allow each harbor to practice planting and retrieving mines. Their hoisting equipment enabled them to handle the heavy mines and anchors, but mine planting in bad weather was hard, dangerous work that required teamwork and careful attention to detail.

In addition to the mine planter, distribution box boats (L-boats) were smaller boats that held the distribution box while it was being attached to the cables. A boom hoisted the assembled distribution box over the bow and lowered it into the water. Mine yawls, even smaller vessels, ferried ropes, cables, etc. from the mine planter to the distribution box boat or to shore. In reality, harbor defenses often had to make do with improvised vessels, including barges and chartered ferryboats. After having planted the mines in an intensive operation at or before the start of hostilities, the mine command manned searchlights and rapid-fire batteries to protect the mine fields.

Fire control and position finding

Fire control was the heart of the coast artillery. More than anything else, it made the difference between a devastating hit and just a loud noise. The meaning of "fire control" evolved during the 65 years of the Modern Era, but in its later, broadest sense, it was all the factors that went into directing the fire, including the discovery and identification of targets, the assignment of targets to specific units, the selection of ammunition, and when to fire.

Also included was the complex procedure to predict the future location of the target, calculate the firing data, and sending it to the guns to enable them to strike the target at the predicted point. This long, complex process had to be rapid and precisely accurate.

Endicott-Taft fire control

Before the Endicott-Taft period, the artillery had virtually no fire-control equipment or technique. Short ranges, slow targets, and the absence of communication all worked against any fire-control system. Individual gunners aimed their guns under the loose supervision of an officer, who would at most point out targets. The gunner, operating virtually autonomously, mentally calculated the gun's azimuth and elevation, allowing for wind and drift.

With the introduction of breech-loading cannon, the range of artillery increased markedly, just as warship speed increased with the final triumph of steam over sail. The artillery needed some effective means to direct and control the new guns, but it was far from clear what that would turn out to be.

The first step was to locate the target's position. Two separated observers with devices for measuring the azimuth to the target could determine its location, if the observers' locations were accurately established; they took their readings at the same instant, and transmitted the information to the battery rapidly. In the 1890s, the telephone was inefficient, the telegraph required expensive operators, and visual signaling was too slow. For about a decade, beginning around 1895, engineers and artillerymen struggled with these problems as the army's Signal Corps pushed to develop the necessary means of communications.

In the first decade of the 20th century, this started to come together, with telautographs to reproduce writing at a distant receiver. Despite early technical difficulties, within a few years they operated satisfactorily. Meanwhile, the Signal Corps introduced the first telephones specifically designed for coast artillery work. At the end of the decade, these telephones were so efficient that the artillery abandoned the more complex telautograph. By this time, after the Taft Report, the "standard system" of fire control had been developed and the harbor-by-harbor installation that spanned more than a decade had begun.

The first step in the process was the identification of a hostile ship. At night, searchlights were essential. The observers passed this information to the fire commander and harbor defense commander, who assigned the target or targets to specific batteries. Before the target came within range, observers would begin to track the target to determine its location and path by triangulation, either vertical or horizontal.

With the vertical system, a depression position finder (DPF) at a known height above the water – either

BELOW Fire-control station with a depression position finder on a pedestal and an azimuth instrument on a tripod for adjusting fire. (US Army Casemate Museum)

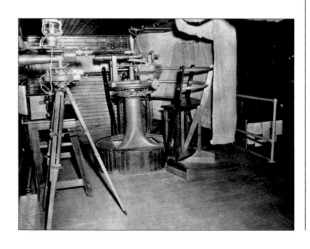

ABOVE Plotting a firing solution in one of the plotting rooms for the 12in. mortars at batteries Andersons-Ruggles, Fort Monroe, VA. Note the combination of telephone, voice tubes, and mechanical indicators to communicate with fire-control stations and mortar pits. (US Army Casemate Museum)

high ground or tower – used a finely machined and calibrated instrument to calculate the distance to the target by measuring the small angle the telescope was depressed when pointed at the target. The horizontal system required two observing (base end) stations at each end of a measured horizontal line. When observers took readings on a target at exactly the same time, its location could be plotted graphically on a board.

Both systems had advantages and disadvantages. The vertical-base system required costlier instruments and needed careful adjustment for tide and atmospheric refraction. In addition, the accuracy of the DPF was limited by the height of the instrument, an increasing problem as ranges became longer. The horizontal-base system was more accurate at longer ranges and less dependent on precise adjustment, but required twice as many observers, as well as a more complex communication system. In addition, if the two observers tracked different targets, the results were worthless.

After a period of experimentation, both systems were used. Although the horizontal-base system predominated, the emphasis depended in part on the availability of high sites for observers, and usually one base end station of a pair was given a DPF. Tying the entire network together, a time-interval system provided a common time standard by ringing bells simultaneously at fixed intervals in observing stations, plotting rooms, and gun emplacements.

A reader at each station was directly connected by telephone to the battery plotting room, where the plotting-arm setters set the azimuths from the two stations on the arms of the plotting board. This large, graphic representation of the area was precisely scaled, with the battery and observing stations carefully located. Arms from the observing stations were each set for the observed azimuth of the target (or in the case of a vertical-base system, the azimuth and range from one station). The intersecting point represented the target, and the distance and range from the designated directing point of the battery could be quickly measured on a third (gun) arm.

From a series of such points at precise intervals, the speed and course of the target could be estimated. From this, they would determine where the target would be after the gun had been fired, allowing for the time of flight of the projectile. This data now had to be fine-tuned. Gun elevation for a given range was based on standard conditions seldom duplicated, so the elevation was adjusted for the temperature of the powder, the density and humidity of the air, the exact weight of the projectile, wind strength and direction, and the previous performance of the same lot of powder. Azimuth had to be adjusted

RIGHT Inside the plotting room for Battery Pennsylvania, Oahu, HI, in March 1945. Note the M-4 plotting board and M-1 gun data computer. (NARA Still Pictures)

for wind and drift from the gyroscopic action of the spinning projectile. All this had to be rapid, calm, and precise.

The form of the data then sent to the guns depended on the "case" being used. In case one, the gunner determined his own azimuth and estimated his range. In case two, the plotting room supplied the range and the gunner set his sight on the target, with the deflection, or azimuth correction, from the plotting room. In case three, the plotting room supplied both range and azimuth, which was set on the azimuth circle at the base of the carriage. Guns normally used case two, while mortars, positioned out of view of the target, always used case three, or indirect fire.

An additional option was the self-contained range finder (SCRF), the primary means for determining range for smaller, rapid-fire batteries and a supplemental means for larger ones. The seacoast artillery replaced coincidence range finders (CRF) stereoscopic range finders during World War II. In effect a miniature baseline in a tube 9 to 21ft long, SCRF were quick and provided an alternative if the primary fire-control system should be disabled, but their accuracy declined with range and so could not be relied on by long-range guns.

With the deflection set on the sight, the sight aimed at the target, and the carriage at the proper elevation, the shell and moving target should meet. In reality, the first round was unlikely to be exactly on target, and subsequent shots would have to be observed and adjusted, a process known as spotting. Both the guns and the fire-control system were much more accurate in azimuth than in range, so range was the critical element, the adjustment of which was a complex, technical process.

This standard system was installed at a few harbor defenses each year, for more than a decade. Meanwhile, mechanical devices, analog computers, simplified the calculations and decreased the chance of error. This, of course, exaggerates the uniformity. Different harbor defenses received the standard system at different times, while officers were encouraged to experiment and invent fire-control devices. Disputes flourished as to the best methods, and the *Journal of United States Artillery* contains many articles on the subject. While the level of discussion eased during the second decade of the century, fire control remained a fluid subject, always with room for new ideas and devices.

Fire control between the World Wars

World War I introduced both new techniques and new problems. Firing at longer ranges and higher angles of elevation revealed problems, particularly with projectiles, unnoticed with flat trajectories. In addition, new long-range batteries could engage targets beyond the horizon, with times of flight up to a minute and a half, during which time the target might move well over a mile. This meant predicting the location of the target at impact time was much more difficult. On the positive side, aircraft and balloons had effectively adjusted fire on land, and offered some hope they might be adaptable for seacoast firing.

The 1920s were a period of retrenchment, and little money was available for improvements. Nonetheless, the Coast Artillery Board, the research and development agency for the chief of coast artillery, continued to investigate fire

LEFT Battery Kirkpatrick's (Wilridge) two-level battery commander's station with SCR-296 radar antenna on its roof. (NARA Still Pictures)

Fire-control tower

The primary function of these stations was to track targets and provide range and direction data for nearby coastal batteries. A typical station had two types of observing instruments, shown in the top right inset. The larger depression position finder could measure the range to the target by itself. The smaller azimuth instrument could work in conjunction with an instrument in another station, or it could be used for spotting, to adjust the fire of the battery. The main illustration shows the camouflaged fire-control tower at Halibut Point, Rockport, MA, which was one of few sites that served two harbor defenses at the same time. The tower today is open to the public as part of Halibut Point State Park.

LEFT Three rare fire-control stations on steel towers survive at Smith Island, Cape Charles, VA, as seen from 200ft in 2000. The two concrete stations have weathered the elements better than the steel station in the center. These stations supported batteries at forts John Custis and Story at the entrance to Chesapeake Bay. (McGovern Collection)

control and to work with private manufacturers on the development of analog fire-control computers. Kite balloons assigned to coast artillery posts in the early 1920s proved less helpful than had been hoped, and were phased out. On the other hand, experiments with aircraft observers, both army and navy, showed promise, but a great deal of joint training would be necessary before they produced practical benefits. The Ordnance Department tried to improve the consistency of the powder and hence the range, but the difficulty in tracking the target and predicting its path at long ranges remained.

At the same time, the coast artillery was now employing new mobile armament: railway guns and 155mm field guns left over from World War I. Their very mobility negated the advantage of fixed, precisely located fire-control positions. Further problems included the need for a mobile time-interval device and for gun sights suited for direct fire at moving targets. In the 1920s and 30s, coast artillery officers and NCOs, coordinated by the Coast Artillery Board, slowly dealt with these problems.

BELOW A rare surviving Endicott-Taft fire-control tower at Fort Mott State Park, Salem, NJ, in 1989. The steel column in the center of the tower encloses a concrete pier to isolate the fire-control instrument from any motion of the tower. (McGovern Collection)

Fire control in World War II

In the 1930s, a number of devices were perfected: new telephones, DPFs, mobile time-interval devices, panoramic sights, and a wide range of plotting-room devices. However, penury generally prevented their manufacture in volume until war began to loom around 1940 and money finally began to become available. Then the Ordnance Department and Signal Corps struggled to manufacture and issue devices, which were produced one at a time by skilled workmen and allotted to specific forts or batteries long before they were completed. Some devices, such as plotting boards, had to be custom made for specific battery locations. Through most of World War II, batteries were slowly equipped with the newest fire-control devices.

The history of fire control in World War II divides into two periods, although the timing varied for different harbors and even batteries. In the first period, new equipment, improvements of older equipment, was issued as fast as it could be manufactured. Some equipment merely comprised older items modified for easier production. A new generation of sights,

observing instruments, plotting boards, telephones, and a large number of plotting-room boards and devices all served to improve the accuracy and efficiency of fire control.

Meanwhile, however, development was under way on two devices that would bring fundamental changes during the second period. The army had long desired a computer to eliminate the time-consuming and error-prone series of calculations that produced firing data. During the 1920s and 30s, the Coast Artillery Board, working closely with the Ordnance Department, tested and critiqued models developed by private firms. The army, however, had no money to push the development, and the need for antiaircraft computers, or directors, was more pressing. Taking advantage of antiaircraft computers, two quite different seacoast computers, the M1 and the M8, were developed. These computers required local charts and were custom made for each site. Both the M1 and the M8 were successful, although batteries retained their plotting boards and accessories in case the computers failed.

The M1 gun data computer (GDC) was produced first, in 1942, for 12in. and 16in. guns. It was mechanical, with only minor electric functions. Data from observing stations or radar, and ballistic data input by dials and cranks, produced a predicted future target position and computed firing data. Spotting could be used to correct the firing data.

The M8 GDC, on the other hand, was for guns up to eight inches. Based on experience gained developing the M9 antiaircraft director, the M8 was electrical, using an array of vacuum tubes. Unlike the M1, it was not a single unit, but had a separate predictor, receiver, line balancer, and power unit. Different models were used with 6in., 8in., 90mm, and 155mm guns.

The computers, despite their advantages, did not revolutionize fire control. Radar did. Invented and developed jointly by British, Canadian, and American scientists, it bounced radio waves off a target and measured the time lapse back to the set. With the orientation of the antenna, this gave the range and azimuth to the target. The advantages were tremendous. Most importantly, the guns were finally no longer dependent on visibility. Rain, fog, haze, or night no longer prevented target acquisition and targeting. Increased accuracy at longer ranges was an additional benefit.

BELOW Two round fire-control towers survive at Dewey Beach, DE. These 1943 towers supported batteries at Fort Miles, DE. (McGovern Collection)

The concept was simple, but there were significant technical hurdles to overcome, the greatest being generating enough power at high frequency, corresponding to a short wavelength. The CAC's interest in radar dated from 1937, but antiaircraft radar had higher priority and it was several years before the first surface radar set was standardized. A number of antiaircraft and surface sets were developed during the war, and some sets of one type were used in the other role. Essentially, surface radar was of two types: gun laying and surveillance.

The first gun-laying set was delivered in April 1942, to new batteries 6in. or larger. With a 40cm wavelength, it was typically mounted in a cylindrical housing atop a 100ft steel tower. While successful, its long wavelength limited its accuracy and made it vulnerable to jamming. In addition, it could not track multiple targets. It was eventually credited with tracking capital ships at 40,000 yds and smaller ships at 20,000 yds.

Surveillance radar warned of multiple targets. The first of this type had a 10.7cm wavelength and could track multiple targets at a maximum range of 90,000 yds. It was accurate within 25 yds at 35,000 yds. A mobile version had five times the power and consequently greater range. Mobile 10cm sets were used with 90mm AMTB and 155mm seacoast batteries.

Wartime development culminated postwar, with 3cm sets accurate to 10 yds at 50,000 yds. The combination of radar, computers, and other new accessories greatly increased accuracy by day or night, in good weather or bad, and at much longer ranges.

Recommended reading

Berhow, Mark A., ed., *American Seacoast Defenses: A Reference Guide*, 2nd Ed. (Bel Air, MD: CDSG Press, 2004).

Browning, Robert S., *Two If By Sea: The Development of American Coastal Defense Policy* (Westport, CT: Greenwood, 1953).

Coast Artillery Journal, 1922–47, Fort Monroe, VA.

Coast Defense Journal, previously published as *CDSG News* and the *Coast Defense Study Group Journal*.

Conn, Stetson, Rose Engelman, and Bryon Fairchild, *Guarding the United States and Its Outposts* (Washington, DC: Center for Military History, 1962).

Floyd, Dale E., *Defending America's Coasts: 1775–1950, A Bibliography* (Washington: Office of the Chief of Engineers, 1997).

Hines, Frank T. and Franklin W. Ward, *The Service of Coast Artillery* (New York: Goodenough & Woglom Co., 1910; reprint, Bel Air, MD: CDSG Press, 1997).

Journal of the United States Artillery, 1892–1922, Fort Monroe, VA.

Lewis, Emanuel Raymond, *Seacoast Fortifications of the United States: An Introductory History* (Washington: Smithsonian, 1970).

McGovern, Terrance, *The American Harbor Defenses of the Panama Canal* (McLean, VA: Redoubt Press, 1999).

McGovern, Terrance C. and Mark A. Berhow, *American Defenses of Corregidor and Manila Bay 1898–1945*, Osprey Fortress Series No. 4 (Oxford, UK: Osprey, 2003).

US Congress, House Exec. Doc. No. 49, 49th Cong., 1st Sess., *Report of the Board on Fortifications or Other Defenses Appointed by the President of the United States under the Provisions of the Act of Congress Approved March 3, 1885* [The Endicott Report] (GPO, 1886).

US Congress, Senate Doc. No. 248, 59th Cong., 1st Sess., *Report of the National Coast Defense Board Appointed by the President of the United States by Executive Order, January 31, 1905* [The Taft Report](GPO, 1906).

US War Dept., Annual Reports of the Secretary of War, Reports of the Chief of Artillery, 1902–07; Chief of Coast Artillery, 1908–37; Chief of Engineers, 1886–1920, and Chief of Ordnance, 1886–1920 (GPO).

US War Dept., *Drill Regulations for Coast Artillery, United States Army* (GPO, 1898, 1909, and 1914).

US War Dept., Field Manual FM 4-15, *Seacoast Artillery Fire Control and Position Finding* (GPO, 1940).

US War Dept., *Manual for Submarine Mining* (GPO, 1912).

US War Dept., Technical Manual TM 4-210, *Coast Artillery Weapons and Matériel* (GPO, 1940) and *Seacoast Artillery Weapons*, (GPO, 1944; reprint, Bel Air, MD: CDSG Press, 1995).

US War Dept., Chief Signal Officer, Signal Corps Manual No. 8, *Apparatus Supplied by the Signal Corps to Coast Artillery Posts for Fire Control and Direction* (GPO, 1906) and *Installation and Maintenance of Fire Control Systems at Seacoast Fortifications* (GPO, 1914).

US War Dept., Corps of Engineers, "Reports of Completed Batteries," various dates, 1903-18, NARA, Washington, DC, Record Group 77, General Correspondence, 1894–1923, Entry 103.

US War Dept., Office of the Chief of Engineers, Harbor Defense Notebooks, c. 1922, NARA, Washington, DC, Record Group 77, Coast Defense Fortification File, 1898–1920, Entry 220.

US War Dept., Ordnance Dept., *American Coast Artillery Matériel* (GPO, 1923; reprint, Bel Air, MD: CDSG Press, 2001).

Williford, Glen and Terrance McGovern, *Defenses of Pearl Harbor and Oahu 1907–50*, Osprey Fortress Series No. 8 (Oxford, UK: Osprey, 2003).

Winslow, Eben Eveleth, *Notes on Seacoast Fortification Construction*, Occasional Papers No. 61, US Army Engineer School (GPO, 1920; reprint, Bel Air, MD: CDSG Press, 1994).

The authors also relied on documents in the National Archives and Records Administration (NARA), in Washington, DC, and College Park, MD. Anyone interested in more information on these sources is invited to contact the authors at bollingsmith@hotmail.com.

Glossary

Definitions evolved over time. These are generally correct, but may not be precise for every specific date.

Azimuth   The horizontal angle to an object, measured clockwise from south.

Azimuth instrument   A telescopic instrument to measure azimuths.

Balanced pillar   A carriage whose gun remained above the parapet for loading and firing but below the parapet for concealment.

Barbette carriage   A carriage whose gun remained over the parapet for loading and firing.

Baseline   A horizontal line of known length, direction, and position, between two base end stations, used for position finding.

Battery   One or more guns or mortars grouped to fire on a single target, along with the entire structure for their emplacement, protection, and service. Also, a unit of artillery troops equivalent to a company. The meaning must be determined by the context.

Cannon   Artillery weapon to throw a projectile by the force of exploding powder. See *gun* and *mortar*.

Carriage   The mechanism for supporting a gun or mortar tube and pointing it in azimuth and elevation.

Casemate   Originally a vaulted room. By extension, a gun position with overhead cover. Also, the control room for a submarine mine system.

Coast Defense   An administrative and tactical unit assigned to the defense of a specific harbor. In 1925, renamed Harbor Defense.

Controlled submarine mine   A watertight metal case containing explosive, with a means for electrically firing the mine from shore.

Disappearing carriage   A carriage that raised a gun above the parapet for firing, recoiling back and down, behind the parapet, for loading.

DPF   Depression Position Finder; an elevated instrument that measured the azimuth to a target and determined the distance by measuring the angle down to the target from the horizontal.

Elevation   The vertical angle of the gun.

Emplacement   That part of a battery that pertained to the position, protection, and service of one gun, mortar, or group of mortars.

Endicott-Taft   The program for defending the harbors of the United States and its possessions based on the 1886 report of the Endicott Board, and amended by the 1906 report of the Taft Board. The system that resulted was the Endicott-Taft System.

Fire command   A tactical unit of one or more batteries that covered the same general water area.

Fire control   A term that came to mean all the functions of locating and identifying a target, assigning targets, and determining the firing data to allow the guns to hit the target.

Fuze   A device in a projectile to explode the bursting charge.

GPF   *Grande Puissance Filloux*; a French 155mm gun on a wheeled field carriage. Also manufactured in America, it was widely used in the CAC.

Group   The name given to the fire command after World War I.

Groupment   A tactical command within a Harbor Defense, containing two or more groups.

Gun   Long cannon used for direct fire at low elevations and high velocities.

Harbor Defense   See *Coast Defense*.

HECP   Harbor Entrance Control Post; a joint army–navy center to control access to defended harbors.

Loading platform   The portion of the emplacement the gunners stand on to load the gun.

Magazine   A room or structure for storing powder, primers, or fuzes. Also an entire structure to store ammunition.

Masking parapet mount   A proprietary balanced pillar mount.

Modern Era   1885–1950; the period of harbor defenses using steel breech-loading weapons in concrete and earth batteries.

Mortar   Short cannon for high-angle fire at low velocities.

Non-tactical   Supporting not directly used in battle, such as barracks, storehouses, and utilities. Non-tactical structures were the responsibility of the Quartermaster Corps until 1941, after that, the Corps of Engineers.

Parapet   The part of a battery that protected the gun and personnel from frontal fire. During the Modern Era, this was concrete and earth.

Pedestal mount   A type of barbette carriage with concentric recoil in a cradle, for fixed guns between three and six inches.

Plotting room   A room where the position of the target was determined and firing data computed for the gun.

Primer   A device that ignited the propelling charge in a cannon.

Projectile   A missile thrown from a cannon.

Rifle   As used by the artillery, a gun.

Sub-caliber   A small gun attached to a larger gun for practice firing.

Tactical   Directly used in battle, such as batteries, searchlights, fire-control buildings, and mine structures. Tactical structures were the responsibility of the Corps of Engineers.

Telautograph   An electrical device for transmitting writing to a distant receiver. Used by the coast artillery, 1902–10.

Torpedo   An earlier term for a subsurface explosive, including submarine mines.

Traverse   The part of a battery that protected the gun and personnel from flanking fire.

Radar   RAdio Detection And Ranging: an electronic system that measures distance and direction to an object by the reflection of radio waves.

Zone   In mortar fire, the range with a given powder charge, between the minimum and maximum elevation.

Abbreviations

AMTB   Anti-Motor Torpedo Boat
BC   Barbette Carriage
BCLR   Barbette Carriage, Long Range
BCN   Battery Construction Number
BLM   Breech-Loading Mortar
BLR   Breech-Loading Rifle
BP   Balanced Pillar carriage
CAC   Coast Artillery Corps, 1907–50
DC   Disappearing Carriage
DPF   Depression Position Finder
GDC   Gun Data Computer
MC   Mortar Carriage
MP   Masking Parapet (carriage)
MR   Military Reservation
NCO   Non-Commissioned Officer
NPS   National Park Service
NRA   National Recreation Area

Index

Figures in **bold** refer to illustrations

1870 Program 11
1940 Modernization Program 4, 14, 15, 41

Abbott, Col. Henry L. 31, 46, 49
Abbott-quad mortar batteries 31, 33, **34**
American Civil War 10-11, 46
ammunition 45
anti-motor torpedo boat (AMTB) batteries
16, **43**
Artillery Corps 13, 48

barbette carriages **11**, 13, 32, 33, 38, 39
batteries
anti-motor torpedo boat (AMTB) 16, **43**
casemated **15**, **20**, 40–1
Endicott-Taft 30, 33, 36–7
mortar 31, **34**
post-World War I 38–40
Spanish-American War 30–1
World War II 40–4
Bernard, Gen. Simon 10
Board of Engineers for Fortifications 4, 10,
21, 46, 57
breech-loading guns 30, 31
breech-loading mortars (BLM) 12, 30, 31
Buffington-Crozier disappearing carriages 13,
30, 32, **36**, 37

cannons 10, **11**
Castillo de San Marcos 9
Castle William 9
Cleveland, Grover 12
coast artillery companies 24
Coast Artillery Corps (CAC) 5, 13–14, 16,
39, 40, 48, 56
inter-war years 19
pre-World War I 17–18
World War I 18–19
World War II 19–20
coast artillery districts 24
Coast Defense Study Group (CDSG) 59
"Columbiads" 10
Corps of Engineers 11, 12, 13, 26, 29, 48

Debange screw breech 30
depression position finders (DPF) 51–2
Dewey Beach **56**
disappearing carriages 13, **30**, 32–3, **35**, **36**, 38

electricity 33
Endicott, William C. 12
Endicott System 4, 12–13
Endicott-Taft System (1885–1915) 4, 13–14
battery design 30, 33, 36–7
fire control 51–3, **55**
forts 26, 28
mortar and gun design 30
searchlights 57

fire control
Endicott-Taft 51–3, **55**
inter-war years 53–5
stations **51**

towers 54, **55**, 56
World War II 55–6
First System (1794–1806) 9
Fort Amezquita: Battery Reed 44
Fort Burnside: BCN 213 **29**
Fort Canby 39
Fort Casey 60
Battery Worth **12**
Fort Columbia 60
Fort Dawes 27
Fort DeSoto 60
Fort Drum 32, 38
Fort Duvall **59**
Fort Flagler 60
Searchlight Station No. 13 **57**
Fort Funston **15**
Battery Davis 40, **60**
Battery Townsley 40
Fort Grant **42**
Fort Hancock **26**, 60
Battery Gunnison/New Peck **14**
Battery Kingman **36**, **45**
Battery McCook-Reynolds 33
Battery Potter 37, **38**
Fort H.G. Wright **23**
Fort John Custis: BCN 227 **25**
Fort MacArthur 60
Batteries Osgood and Farley **16**
Fort Michie: barracks **28**
Fort Miles 60
Battery 21 **22**
Fort Mills 60
Fort Monroe **10**, 60
Battery Anderson **21**, **31**
Battery DeRussey **17**, **30**
Battery Irwin **37**
Battery Parrott **17**
plotting rooms **52**
Fort Mott **11**, 38, 60
fire-control towers **55**
Fort Moultrie **11**, 60
Fort Pickens 60
Battery Cullum **19**
Battery Pensacola **35**
Battery Worth **31**
BCN 234 **19**
Fort Rosecrans
Battery McGrath **37**
Searchlight Station No. 6 **58**
Fort Ruckman: Battery Gardner **39**
Fort Scott
Battery Chamberlain **13**
Battery Godfrey **30**
Fort Stevens **9**, 39, 60
Fort Story **20**
Battery Walke **41**
Battery Worcester 41
Fort Sumter: Battery Huger **36**
Fort Taylor **18**
Fort Terry: BCN 217 **25**
Fort Tilden: Battery Harris **5**
Fort Wadsworth 60
Fort Warren 60
Fort Wetherill **47**, 60
Fort Wint: mine casemate **48**
Fort Worden 60

forts
Endicott-Taft 26, 28
Third System 26
World War II 29

General Ord (mine planter) **46**
gun data computers (GDC) 56

harbor defense
1916–36 14
1937–45 14
1945–50 14, 16
hoists 32, 33

Krupp sliding breech 30

land defenses 24–5

mine planters **46**, 50
"mobilization" buildings 29
Modern Era 4, 5, 21–5
modified theater-of-operations (MTO)
buildings 29

National Guard 14, 19, 25, 29, 40
National Land Defense Board 25
National Park Service (NPS) 59
Navesink Highland Military Reservation:
Battery Lewis **16**, **20**

Oahu 39, 40, 42
plotting room **52**
Ordnance Corps 12
Ordnance Department 12–13, 30, 31, 37, 38,
39, 48, 55
Organized Reserve 14, 19

Panama Canal 44
"Panama mounts" 40

Quartermaster Corps 26, 28, 29

radar 56
railway artillery **22**, 39–40, 42
range finders 53
rapid-fire guns 37
"Rodman" guns 10, 11, **11**, 31
Roosevelt, Theodore 13

searchlights 57–8
Second System (1807–15) 9–10
Signal Corps 26, 51, 55
Smith Island, Cape Charles 55
Spanish-American War 13
emergency batteries 30–1
submarine mines 11, 12, 13, 24, 46–50

Taft, William H. 13
Taylor-Raymond hoists 32, **32**
Third System (1816–67) 4, 10–11, 26
Totten, Bvt. Lt. Col. Joseph 10

War of 1812 4, 10
Watervliet Arsenal **24**

Zalinski dynamite guns 38